Now *THAT* Wasn't in the Brochure

ROSALIE DICKSON BOILEAU

ISBN: 098685610X
ISBN 13: 978-0986856105

Some names and identifying details have been changed to protect the
privacy of individuals.

IN LOVING MEMORY OF TROY

JAMES BOILEAU

FEBRUARY 4, 1967 TO AUGUST 5, 2008

TROY'S LIFE WAS CUT

TRAGICALLY SHORT. HIS DEATH

HAS SPURRED ME TO STOP

TALKING ABOUT IT, AND TO JUST DO IT.

Dedication

I dedicate this book to my husband Bob. He has followed me, sometimes reluctantly, to the edges of the earth, and more than once, he has kept me from jumping off.

He is my voice of reason, a guardian angel who wraps his loving arms around me and keeps me grounded as common sense flings on its jacket and stomps out the door like a jilted lover.

Table of Contents

Acknowledgments

My heartfelt appreciation goes to my cousin Arlene who said that if I didn't write the damn book, she would.

I must send a world of thanks to my sister Dorothy for her endless hours spent editing, her gentle criticism, and her words of encouragement. Her advice has really helped my work blossom into something of which I am proud.

I should like to thank Joyce Jackson who sat at a table in her cabin overlooking the sea as she corrected my punctuation and grammar, and to Stewart Jackson for his enthusiasm and eye for detail.

Thank-you to Barb for her time spent editing and bringing to my attention that the correct spelling is 'polka dot' and not 'poke-a-dot'.

Loving hugs to my friends and family who tell me when they read my emails home they feel as if they are there with me. It is these continuing comments, which have kept me focused and writing, and rest assured you are there with me.

I must thank my friend Stuart for inadvertently providing me with my title. We were having cocktails on the beach, at Sundowners Bar in Roatan, and he was relaying a story about the island when he said, "Now THAT Wasn't in the Brochure!" and I knew it was my missing title.

My heart aches for my children, Robert and Michelle, and my grandchildren, Alec, Evan, Wesley, Marenda and Kaiden, who indulge my absences and never guilt me for not being there on a birthday or at Easter or on Christmas morning. They willingly sacrifice their needs for mine, a gift I hope I can somehow repay.

Lastly, I must thank my lover and steadfast fan, Bob, for his never-ending encouragement. He tells me that the book is an exciting read. "I want to know what happens next, and I was there!"

Prologue

"In the end, stories are what's left of us, we are no more than the few tales that persist."

- Salman Rushdie
The Moor's Last Sigh

I once met a woman, on a dive boat, in Tonga. She was in her early seventies, tiny and thin with short-cropped salt and pepper hair, and a sinewy weathered body. We chatted as the boat raced towards the reef. She was travelling the world alone for six months, going wherever the next adventure took her. When I marveled at the fact she was travelling solo at her age she answered with this, "Any grandmother can sit at home in a rocking chair and knit booties for their grandbabies, but how many grandmothers can tell their grandchildren they have snorkeled the Great Barrier Reef, or spent Christmas morning at church, with the King of Tonga?" She had missed birthdays, Christmases, births, deaths, and other special occasions. It was at this moment that I realized it was not that she didn't love her family; that was evident in the way she spoke of them, but she also loved herself.

There is a big difference between 'going on vacation' and 'travelling'. Most people envision a vacation as two weeks at an all-inclusive resort in Mexico, the Caribbean, or Hawaii. Sand, sun, surf and that vitally important cold beer, delivered by a local who walks a long journey at day's end, home to his large family. The server is religious, most often Catholic, poor and uneducated. He gets paid little but he is glad to have the work the resort provides. Others are lined up behind him to take his job. The meager tips he receives from the sun-scorched tourists, feed and house his family better than if he were sweating seven days a week in the fields. People rarely look at his face. His English is poor, but occasionally he makes a connection, a friend.

I yearn to be that friend. Several times, I have succeeded in leaping the cultural chasm by nurturing a fleeting chance and feeding a melding, hindered by language but fused by a shared humanity.

My life's passion is to travel and I have been fortunate enough to be able to do so. Bob and I plan a yearly, two-month, trip to far and exotic places. Our decision, as to a destination, is often determined on a whim. Something as little as, "I've always wanted to go to…or this place looks interesting… or gee there are cheap airfares to… or the weather should be good there this time of year… or I bet this place has good scuba diving."

People often say, "I wish we could live the life Bob and you do." To which I reply, "You can! You just have to decide it is what you want, and do it!"

We love adventure but there I go, wrapping Bob into it. Often I think he follows along just to keep me safe. I am a self-proclaimed adrenaline junkie, a thrill seeker, and a kid at heart. I have suffered all of my life from 'Peter Pan Syndrome'. I never want to grow up. Despite turning fifty-five this year, I am still able to maintain this flight of fancy until a mirror, unexpectedly, catches me off guard. In defiance, I stick my tongue out at the old lady staring back and she soon disappears. I am also ashamed to admit that I succumb to peer-pressure, something Bob, thankfully, does not. This is not a good trait when the adventures I seek usually attract twenty-five year olds. Oft times my body feels bruised, battered, and broken: however, no one will ever know.

What I love the most about travelling are the people we meet, not only the locals, who are a huge part of the experience, but the travellers. People from all over the world, of all ages and all walks of life, interesting people, who often leave me feeling inadequate and speechless. They are the doctors, the lawyers, the engineers, the nurses, and the teachers. They speak three languages and are semi fluent in a fourth. They have travelled to corners of the world I have never even heard of. They know the history and economics of every place to which they have been and have done humanitarian work there. They have adopted third world children who are now young adults going to universities back in Canada, the States, and Germany. Well, you get my drift. They humble and inspire me. I tell myself, "This year I will learn Spanish. I will write my book. I will exercise every day, and I will be a better friend!"

We also meet the wanderers and the nomads. Young people of no fixed address, sleeping six to a dorm in buggy, vermin infested hostels, and eating questionable food from roadside vendors for pennies a meal. Sporting greasy hair or dirty dreadlocks, they wear Teva sandals, soiled and tattered clothes, and lug scuffed stained backpacks bulging at the seams with damp moldy towels and worn leather hiking boots hanging from them.

Every single one of these adventurers is unique with stories to tell, stories of the 'tourists trail', which really does exist. Something which amazes me, and proves the existence of 'the trail', is the fact that when you travel, in any given country, you often run into the same people, sometimes weeks later, with a dog-eared Lonely Planet clutched in their fist. The encounter could be in a greasy local restaurant, or a street market, at a temple, or on a bus. The, "Haven't I seen you someplace before?" conversation, the connection making you fast friends, friendships that can last a lifetime.

Before we travel, I go to the Dollar Store and buy baseball caps, three dollars each, in red, navy, or black with 'Canada' emblazoned on the front. We dole them out to tour guides or taxi drivers as a thank-you, along with their tips. The recipients are always grateful and we have received many crooked, stained tooth or toothless, grins in return.

I always save one of these caps for Bob to wear. It serves two purposes. One, it lets everyone know that we are proudly Canadian and two, it opens up conversations with a multitude of people. The conversations usually start with, "What part of Canada are you from?" The answer is invariably, "British Columbia." "Yes,

but where in British Columbia?" "We are near Vancouver."
"Oh, but where, near Vancouver?" "Gibsons." "Really? I am from,
Kelowna...Vernon...Sechelt...Surrey...Calgary...Edmonton."

The connection is made and a friendship is hatched. It is the
best three dollars I have ever spent.

Friends have been telling me for several years, "You have to
write a book. We love your emails. We wait in anticipation for
the next chapter like an episode of a soap opera." I am not sure
whether our adventures are book worthy but I will write it, if only
for friends, family, children, and grandchildren, and to leave a
legacy of adventure, which I hope will inspire them to step out
of their comfort zone.

My emails home often are long and rambling, filled with
errors in spelling and grammar. Each journey produces only a
few episodes worth telling and re-telling. Therefore, I will fashion
my book as short stories, which is often the way I would convey
them to patient friends and family after we have returned home.

Our travels have taken us many places over many years. Every
destination has been unique, and friends often ask, "Would you
go back there again?" We usually say, "No, we have been there.
We have far too many other places on our list which we still need
to see." The only exception is Africa. Africa has imbedded itself
in our hearts and our souls, a symbiosis of sorts where I hope
both parties claim benefit. A massive continent, impossible to
explore in the years we have left, but we are determined to give
it a valiant try. The countries of Africa are immensely diverse: the
people, the economics, the politics, the scenery, and the wildlife.
Africa is an amazing continent and we excitedly anticipate many
return trips.

In many ways, my travel memoir is already written. It fills
the pages of the spiral bound journals in which I scribble with a
religious fervor in planes, trains, buses, boats, airports, jungles,
tents, cabins, and well worn hotel rooms, on sandy beaches,
mountain tops and lake shores. These journals have a magical
way of transporting me back in time. They fill in all of the blank
recesses, which have an insidious way of developing over time

and with age. My mind explodes with sights, sounds, smells and colour. These journals are my most valued possession and the one treasure I would gather up in my arms if my house were on fire.

I hope you enjoy the excitement of our life journey as much as we do.

CHAPTER 1

The Tomboy

My name is Rosalie Dawn Dickson.

At thirteen, I lost my virginity, at sixteen, I was pregnant, and at seventeen, I was married.

Before puberty, I was a tomboy, freckled, with curly strawberry blonde hair, skinned knees, and perpetually dirty fingernails. Innocent and carefree, I built forts in the bushes, scaled tall trees, roller-skated, and rode my heavy tubular bicycle on graveled, oil-blackened roads. I dreamed of becoming an astronaut. After all, my Father told me I could be anything I wanted, if I just wanted it enough. A red rocket radio sat on my bedroom windowsill, its bare antenna wire coiled around my iron bed frame for better reception. Perhaps the aliens would be able to reach me that way. In the dust bunnies underneath my bed, tin tobacco cans with holes punched in their lids housed cocooned caterpillars.

Three months into my pregnancy, my cousin Bobby, then eighteen, was killed in a tragic accident in the United States. Bobby was joy riding with three friends when they slammed full speed into the side of a train at a dark, unmarked, railway crossing. All four were killed instantly.

Tiny and wiry with elfin features, Bobby was a trickster and a showoff. He would do effortless handsprings, to the delight of my Father. I adored my cousin Bobby. It was a hopeless crush. He was the boy I always wished I could be, or if I couldn't *BE* him, then I wanted to marry him. Stubbornly, as a little girl, I refused to realize the impossibility of both of these hormone-fueled fantasies.

My father sired five daughters (one who died in infancy). Bobby was the closest my father would ever get, to having a son. Dad stepped into a fatherly role when his brother Joe died of leukemia six years prior to Bobby's accident. Sadly, Dad was burdened with the job of going down to the United States to identify his nephew's mangled body. The day he identified the body of his brother's son and brought him home to his grieving mother and older sister was one of the most difficult of my fathers' life.

I was devastated by Bobby's death. The day of his funeral, when I went into the bathroom following the service, blood spotted my panties. I desperately wanted the baby I was carrying, yearning to be a mother and a wife, to be needed and wanted. Outwardly, I appeared confident and competent, older than my sixteen years, ready to head off to college and to take on the world. Inwardly, I was terrified of failure and of disappointing my mother and father. I felt like a fraud who would be found out at any moment. I knew I would be safe and cocooned in the domestic life I had secretly planned for myself.

The doctor gave me strict orders to remain in bed with my feet elevated. Terrified, I slept fetal position in my childhood bed. For three days, my Mother hovered hoping I would miscarry. It took me years to forgive her for this, and it wasn't until I was an adult with teenage children of my own that I finally understood.

Doris, my mother, was married at eighteen. Having only achieved a grade nine education, she wanted better for her daughters. I was the golden child, good grades, good girl, she expected me to be the first to complete a higher education. The last thing she wanted for me was pregnancy and dependency on a man. When we girls were in high school, Mom insisted we all take a year of typing. I hated it! I was an academic getting A's. Why should I take typing? "If you need to support yourself, at least you can get a job as a secretary," was her practical but twisted reasoning. Mom died before computers became a household fixture and often I look skyward and thank her for my typing skills.

At the age of forty-nine, my mother died of breast cancer. I was twenty-one. My second child, Michelle, was eighteen months old. Mom's death was wrenchingly difficult. We spent months at her side watching helplessly as cancer ravaged her body. Her left arm swelled to three times its size and blackened lesions oozed foul smelling puss. To this day, I cannot stomach the sickroom smell of Nil Odor.

Our Mother's slow and painful death did give us, and her, the time to say our goodbyes. She bequeathed each of us, in turn, her earthly treasures. I received her 'Old Country Roses' tea set and a hand crocheted doily, Pat her souvenir spoon collection collected over years of travel, Dot her jade ring she bought on a trip to Hong Kong. Mom sent Dot out shopping to Eaton's to buy Lorraine, my youngest sister, a wooden rocking chair to rock her future children; grandbabies Mom would never cradle in her arms. A gold ring with a large pearl and two tiny rubies, she gave to her best friend Stella. Mom said, "Stella is a true friend and if in your lifetime you have only one friend as true as Stella, you are surely blessed."

As she lost her appetite, little could entice Mom to eat. I would go to the bakeshop and bring strawberry custard-filled tarts, which Mom loved, and as she picked at one disinterested, she would say, "Well at least now I don't have to worry about gaining weight, do I?" Her words rattle around in my head every time I berate myself for carrying around extra pounds.

My father, looking at the several bottles of painkillers dotting her bedside table said, "If it was me, I would swallow a whole damn bottle and be done with it." Mom never took this option, bravely giving us precious time we all needed.

The night Mom died, we stood stationed at her hospital bedside trying in vain to keep Death at bay. She was in and out of consciousness and one of the last things she said was, "Well, I will be gone at twelve." We all looked at each other puzzled, thinking it ramblings, caused by too much pain medication. Shortly thereafter, she slipped into a coma. Dad rounded us all up saying, "It is time for us to go home. She is no longer here with us."

After leaving the hospital, we all gathered at Mom and Dad's and slept fitfully on the sofas and the floor. At two minutes after midnight, the telephone rang and the nurse, offering her condolences, reported to Dad that Mom had died at midnight.

My sister Dorothy said, "Mom taught us how to live and now she has taught us how to die."

My Mother loved to travel. Dad worked as a radio technician for Canadian Pacific Airlines and although there was little extra money to spare in the family coffers, his once yearly, free airline passes, allowed us access to far off places. When we travelled, Mom always insisted we wear dresses, carry a purse, and behave like young ladies. "Remember," she would chastise, "you are representing your country."

I am a true believer that something positive results from even the most devastating of tragedies, if only to cause us to pause and re-evaluate the direction of our own lives. Mom did not have the gift of time, making me bound and determined to cherish mine.

My Mother is the reason I travel.

CHAPTER 2

The Catholic Boy

His name is Robert Charles Thomas Boileau.

Bob was raised Catholic, the middle child in a family of seven, five boys, and two girls, where corporal punishment was the norm.

Recently, he shared with me the effect some of the abuse had on his psyche. "Wait until your father gets home," was the threat hanging over someone's head on a daily basis. He said that often his father would take the offender into a bedroom and feign a beating for the benefit of Mother. "Just scream loud and pretend I am beating you," his Dad would instruct tiredly. Bob's oldest brother, Dennis, would often take the blame to spare the younger kids from their Mother's wrath.

Bob grew up in a boxy three-story house built by his father and his grandfather. Steep bare wooden stairs led down to an unfinished concrete basement. The main floor of the house had a living room with a cork floor, a kitchen, a master bedroom, a nursery, and one small bathroom, shared by the entire family of nine. The upstairs had three large bedrooms, one for the girls, Sally and Lorraine, one occupied by his oldest brother Dennis and the third shared by the three younger boys, Bob, Mike and Joe. Baby Timmy inhabited the main floor nursery. Shrubs, at the bottom of their third story window, struggled to survive the nightly 'watering' they received.

When Bob was a small boy, he built a broom and blanket fort in the damp dark basement, illuminating it with a shade-less table lamp. Left unattended, the bare bulb caught the blanket on fire threatening the family home. His mother punished him by holding tightly onto his hand while waving flaming matches on chubby fingers.

When Bob was a young teenager, his father shifted careers. Bob Sr. had been working in a machine shop, rewinding motors, and he worried about his family's financial future, and his health. At work, unprotected, they repaired PCB filled transformers. At forty, Bob Sr. returned to school to become a real estate agent. For years, he was involved in municipal politics as an alderman, and he had a gregarious and outgoing personality. He would do well in his new career, but it would take time. His job and his politics kept him busy days, nights, and weekends, and his absence from the household further frustrated his overwhelmed wife Dolores. The children were expected to do household chores, and the care of the younger siblings was often a burden piled onto the shoulders of the older ones. Bob Sr.'s busy schedule also allowed him to remain emotionally unattached to his brood of seven forcing them to form strong life-lasting bonds with each other.

When his father changed careers, Bob was working nights at the local Safeway store stocking shelves. He would work after school from four to midnight, walk home to sleep, and then go to school the following day. His grades suffered. While his father was attempting to get his new career in full swing, one of Bob's paychecks was spent on groceries to fill an empty refrigerator.

At eighteen, Bob left home after a physical fight with his younger brother Mike, and try as he might to reconcile it, the relationship remains strained to this day.

At nineteen Bob was married to me.

I am the reason Bob travels.

CHAPTER 3

From the Cradle to the Altar

We were married on a sunny October day in the Catholic Church, Our Lady of Assumption. The Catholic Church would sanction our union only on the conditions that we take marriage lessons, and I agree to our children being baptized and raised Catholic. After three evenings of lessons, the young progressive priest, dressed casually in a turtleneck sweater and blue jeans, decided that perhaps we need not come back; this after I excused myself to vomit in his bathroom.

Being married in the church was important to Bob. When we were young newlyweds and we were on vacation, Bob would seek out the local Catholic Church and leaving me nestled in bed, he would go to the early morning Sunday mass, arriving back as I stretched and wiped the sand from my eyes. He never missed a Sunday. Every night Bob would dutifully kneel, cross himself, and pray, hands folded and eyes closed at the edge of our marital bed.

Bob continued to be a devout, practicing Catholic for many years after our marriage and I stood true to my promise to the church. My children attended catechism classes and I sat dutifully and uncomfortably in church when they received their first communion.

Every Sunday, after early mass, both of the kids would arrive home dressed in rumpled and mismatched clothes; Michelle with her strawberry hair in lopsided pigtails, Bobby with an orange juice mustache and an unruly cowlick. I often giggled thinking the old ladies in church must have been clucking, "Look at him, poor sweet man alone with those two little urchins."

Bob's devotion to the church eroded slowly, over time. At a family wedding, a priest he thought to be a trusted friend, snubbed him. He disagreed with the Catholic stance on birth control and the role of women in the church. He recalled being told by older boys when he was a child not to be alone with a priest who was later arrested and charged with pedophilia. He watched as families who struggled to feed their children were pressured at Sunday services to tithe ten percent. He saw his Mother's dedication to the priests and the church go unnoticed. Bob became disillusioned with organized religion but continues, to this day, to practice his religion privately and to be comforted by it. For this, I envy him.

The Boileau boys all have an incredible work ethic, are good fathers, and family men. Although he is now retired, Bob is still the happiest when he is doing physical work. He would joke when we were in business that his favorite job was digging a ditch, saying, "You don't have to think when you are digging a ditch. It is mindless and it feels good to do a hard day's work." This work ethic, coupled with our practical

Our Wedding Day – October 17, 1970

approach to decision making, carried us through many tight times, threading itself through our years in business. We would often enter into a business endeavor looking each other in the eyes and saying, "If the worst possible happens, can we survive it?" If we could answer 'yes' to this question then we would go forward with the risk.

The day we were married we had nothing but each other. Bob had recently been laid off from his job as an electrical apprentice. My pregnant belly uncomfortably stretched the short, off-white, wool dress I wore. My thick, strawberry hair was piled atop my head in coifed curls. I clutched a large bouquet of red roses tightly to my chest. Bob's dad gave him one hundred dollars to buy a new suit to be married in. He chose to wear his old suit, saving the money. He knew we would need it.

We rented a small apartment, built as a nanny suite, in the home of a wealthy couple. The rent was fifty dollars a month with the condition Bob do regular chores around the hobby farm, and transport the two small girls to their private school, in Vancouver, on his way to work.

It was in this apartment, as I slept, early on the morning of March 25th, 1971, my water broke. Eight hours later, I gave birth to a perfect baby boy, Bobby. I named him after his father but also after my beloved deceased cousin.

Bob had an unusual relationship with a Great Auntie. Auntie Ila lived in a mobile home in Maple Ridge. She was in her eighties when we were married. Bob had often spent his weekends as a teenager helping Ila with chores on her two-acre farm. She had chickens, geese, and goats, which she kept in small corrals. Childless, Ila was widowed at a young age when her husband, George, stepped out in front of a bus, committing suicide. She never remarried.

When our son Bobby was an infant, I hated taking him to visit Auntie Ila, but Bob would insist. Auntie was a hoarder and her trailer was filthy. Small pathways had to be negotiated; newspapers and magazines stacked waist high created mazes to her grimy overstuffed chairs. Silver hair swept back in a bun,

Auntie would bounce Bobby playfully on the knee of her soiled housedress while I sat stiffly, trying not to touch or be touched by the filth. Bob was unfazed. She was the beloved woman who fed him and hiked with him in the hills in his youth, and he loved her unconditionally.

On a snowy winter day during one of our regular weekend visits, Auntie Ila shocked us with a proposition. "I have no children of my own Robbie, and I want you to have my property." We were stunned, and Bob immediately refused her generous offer. "You think about this Robbie. I want you to build a house beside the trailer and I will give you some money to get it started. I am getting old and I want you here to help look after me. You are the only one in the family who comes to visit and cares about me."

Ila took us in tow to see her lawyer to have Bob and me added to the title on her property as joint tenants. She also had the lawyer draw up her will leaving all her earthly possessions to her deserving nephew, Robbie.

Several months later, Auntie fell sick, and after much cajoling, we convinced her to see our doctor. The doctor called us into his office to somberly report that Auntie was riddled with cancer. "Go home and make her as comfortable as possible," was the best he could offer.

Ila had known she was dying long before her visit to the doctor, and within months, she was gone.

Young and married, with a toddler, and a baby on the way, Auntie Ila's generosity was life changing and altered the course of our lives. Sadly, it unexpectedly caused a jealous jagged rip in the fiber of our families, a rip that has never fully mended.

In 2010, Bob and I celebrated our 40th wedding anniversary. We have raised our children well, welcomed five grandchildren into the world, operated a successful electrical business, and continue to love each other deeply. We laugh everyday and my heart still catches when he walks through the door after a short absence.

The script of my life - was it written before I was even born? I am excited to know where it will take me before I reach the final act.

CHAPTER 4

Bimini Islands – Bahamas

Twice the Fun…Half the Cost

In November of 1999, Bob and I book a live-a-board dive trip as a late anniversary present to each other. As newly certified divers we had never been on a live-a-board dive trip and we had no inkling as to the adventure about to unfold.

Early November is the end of hurricane season in the Caribbean. Therefore, when I phone the toll free number in Florida to book our trip, I enquire, "What happens if the weather is bad and the trip has to be cancelled?" The young woman, processing our booking at Black Beard Cruises, cheerily replies, "In the ten years we have been doing this trip, we have only cancelled twice." What I didn't realize was that this translated into, "We sail no matter how bad the weather is!"

The package is cheap, only $699 American dollars for a full week of diving, meals included. This, in itself, should have set off some warning bells.

The hotel we had pre-booked for our night in Miami was closed due to a burst water line, and unbeknownst to us they re-booked us into a hotel in a seedy area of Miami Beach. A black night, with dark hulking figures milling about the street corners, Bob and I were afraid to cross the street to a corner gas station to get beverages.

After our unsettling night, we are on board the Pirate Lady tied to a dock in the Miami harbour. Cruise ships, like floating hotels, are moored across the harbour. They welcome their passengers aboard to the calypso beat of steel drums. The Pirate Lady is a 65-foot sailing vessel with basic amenities. When I booked the trip, the young woman asked if I knew what type of trip we were booking. "This isn't the 'Love Boat' I hope ya'all know," she cautioned, with a southern drawl. "There won't be a chocolate waiting on your pillow at night, just so you know."

People are arriving, stowing gear. The cabins are reached by descending a steep ladder-like staircase. Our cabin is small and in the windowless bowels of the forward hull. A shared head, with a hand pump toilet and a small washbasin, sits between cabins at the base of the stairs.

Twenty passengers board the vessel; I am one of only three women. In addition to the passengers, there are six crewmembers, three men, and three women.

At approximately five p.m., Captain Tammy gives us a safety briefing, including instructions for which side of the vessel to stand on when vomiting, ensuring we are upwind. She strongly recommends we take some form of seasick medication, "Even if you have never been seasick before, take something." This is the first indication that it is not going to be 'smooth sailing'. Immediately following the briefing, the cook feeds us a heavy dinner of salty baked ham, complete with veggies and mashed potatoes.

We cast off at eight p.m. in ebony darkness, the wind howling; sailing straight into the heart of the Bermuda Triangle. Bob and I don our new yellow rain suits, jackets and pants, and find a spot to sit on deck mid-ship, hoping it will be the area of least turbulence. We are not asked to wear life jackets, and in hindsight, this amazes me. The wind blows fine spray over the bow and onto the deck. After thirty minutes, the Pirate Lady clears the rock breakwater, thus leaving the safety of the harbour. Huge twelve-foot waves crash over the bow, drenching us to the skin, in spite of our rainwear. It is cold and I curl into a ball, legs tucked up against my chest, fetal position. Bob wraps his arms protectively around me and we sway back and forth, back and forth with each new assault. We turn, staring aft, eyes focused on the heaving moonlit horizon, doing our best to stave off seasickness. The waves crash, the wind howls, the boat shudders. The din obliterates all conversation. Blue and green phosphorescent creatures awash in the waves, shoot across us like laser beams and then slide, landing on the deck, where they scatter like crazed fireflies, slowly extinguishing.

Our travelling companions, the macho men, line up along the rails 'feeding the fish'. I am astounded that no one is washed overboard.

At half past midnight, shivering uncontrollably, teeth chattering, I can no longer stand the cold. Through cupped hands, I yell into Bob's ear, "I am freezing. I can't stay up here any longer." He responds, "I am barely keeping my dinner down. I can't possibly go below deck with you but I will help you to get there." Like drunken sailors, we stagger, our heads bowed into the wind. Gingerly, Bob opens the hatch door leading down to the cabin. A huge wave washes over. Bob gives me a gentle shove and I lurch awkwardly down the steep stairs, stumbling backwards. He slams the door shut just before the next wave. Swallowed up in the darkness I land with a thud at the bottom of the steps.

I desperately need to pee. Wriggling out of my rain pants, I peel down sticky, cold, wet clothes as I am battered to and fro in the phone booth- size head.

Our cabin is on the starboard side of the ship and is shared with a single man. Bob and I have the bottom double bunk and our companion has a single top bunk. After relieving myself, I fall into the cabin and realize our roommate is in. He tells me he has been lying in the bunk since we left the harbour. He recently broke a couple of ribs and he is worried about falling and reinjuring them. I deposit my dripping rain gear on the floor, and I lie in my drenched clothes on our bunk. Resting on bent elbows, I worm out of my sticky wet shorts and panties. Several times my head is driven into the plywood bottom of the upper bunk as the Pirate Lady bucks a wave. I wonder if I will break my neck and be put mercifully out of my misery. Struggling, off comes my t-shirt and soggy bra. Whew! Now I am lying shivering and completely naked, covered only by a thin sheet. A stranger lies inches above me! I am exhausted. It is at this point at which I realize that humanity means more than humility and we are really all one and the same; all in the same proverbial boat. We are just trying to get through the night, vulnerable, cold, and human. At this point nothing separates us, and nothing matters but making it to tomorrow. A thin, tenuous thread attaches us to this life that we are leading on earth.

My body sinks down onto the lumpy foam mattress and I fall blissfully into a deep sleep.

At two a.m., we reach the lee of the Biminis. The Pirate Lady traverses a shallow narrow channel into the harbour *bump, bump, bumping* her keel on the sandy bottom. Shivering and wet, Bob sandwiches his weary body into the bunk beside me, stealing some desperately needed body heat from my now warm and naked body. We doze fitfully until seven-thirty a.m., when we awake to the ringing of the breakfast bell.

Bob and I are novice scuba divers. We took our PADI open water dive course less than a year ago while on a trip to Belize. We naively trust the on-board dive master, Erin. We have not yet learned to question, question, and question. Our frightening experiences on this dive excursion instill this habit in us for the future.

Erin gives us a detailed dive briefing but she is not accompanying us into the water. Everyone is paired with a buddy, most with strangers; Bob and I feel fortunate to have each other.

The water is choppy and the current is strong. It is a tough swim from our entry at the stern of the vessel to the anchor rope at the bow. We descend the anchor line onto a shallow reef. The current seems manageable at thirty feet and we swim around the area, eventually finding our way back to the anchor. Bob checks his air; he still has over half of his tank. So, off we swim again (we later discover the anchor we found, at half a tank, did not belong to our boat but to one of the other two boats of the Black Beard fleet). Soon we are hopelessly lost, under water and in changing terrain. Our only option is to surface. As soon as our heads break the surface, we see we are a long way from the Pirate Lady and drifting fast. We attempt swimming on the surface but soon realize we are losing ground and nearing the end of a small island where the current will be even swifter. Realizing that we need to be rescued, we both thrust our clenched fists high into the air and blast our signaling devices. "Do you think anyone sees us?" I fret. Bob is feeling distressed in the sloppy waves. I tell him, "Keep your regulator in your mouth, help will come." As we drift further from the boat, we watch as the other divers hand up fins and climb the ladder at the stern. No one notices us missing. Eventually, we hear the engine of the dinghy fire up and it is with great relief that we realize help is coming.

Back safely on board, we feel the ridicule of the other divers, the sideways smirks, and the giggles. Bob is unfazed but I am embarrassed, angered, and stung by their smugness.

We sit out dive number two, recuperating, and licking our wounds like beaten dogs.

For dive number three, the Pirate Lady anchors in a howling wind. The current strains the anchor rode. Bob flares, "We don't have to dive in this shit! We can dive anytime we want at home. Why would we dive in this *SHIT*?"

The others cast sideways looks and question condescendingly, "Aren't you guys going on the dive?" The peer pressure begins. Bob remains stoic.

Before the dive is over, seven divers need to be rescued. At the end of the dive, two are in distress at the stern of the boat, fatigued from the current, another diver returns without his buddy. He shrugs walking past Erin when she inquires incredulous, "Where is your buddy?" Divers are drifting everywhere. The outboard engine on the dinghy won't start. A crewmember floats away as he pulls again and again on the useless ripcord; no oars are in his boat. The dinghy engine eventually coughs and spews gassy fumes. It starts and stalls, starts and stalls, as it lurches its way towards the drifting divers.

"Are all the divers accounted for?" someone asks. No, one is still missing; the lost buddy. As we all nervously scan the horizon, Bob spots his shrinking form as he drifts further from the anchored boat. The only reason he is visible is his bright orange safety sausage (a six-foot plastic tube you inflate like a balloon with your regulator). If he had not had this safety sausage as part of his personal gear, we know that without doubt, he would not have been seen. Extremely scary, and a huge lesson learned for Bob and me, this unfortunate event shakes us and we seriously doubt the professionalism of the people to whom we are entrusting our lives.

After a harrowing week, we eventually arrive back in Miami, safe, sound, and on solid ground.

CHAPTER 5

Tonga – South Pacific

The Time She Tried to Kill Me

March of 2003, Bob and I retire from our electrical business. We are young retirees by most standards, Bob at fifty-three and me at forty-nine. However, we have worked extremely hard for thirty years building and running a successful enterprise. Many families have benefited from our hard work; we have put a multitude of young men successfully through electrical apprenticeship programs and have raised two fabulous children, our son Robert, and our daughter Michelle. The time has come to pass the reins to them.

Our success is not due wholly to the electrical business but also to some investments made over the years. These investments, although sometimes scary, have proven profitable. We own three commercial properties paying sufficient in monthly rentals to allow the income to support our travels, and our home is mortgage free.

Our trip this year will take us to Australia, Tonga, and Samoa. Bob has always wanted to see Tonga and it is in Tonga that our courage is truly tested, during a seemingly routine snorkeling trip.

Easter Sunday we book a snorkeling trip through a backpacker hostel in town. We are on one of the islands of Vava'u, the northernmost group of islands in the Tongan archipelago. A grey day, the wind has been blowing hard all morning. Down at the dock we meet our barefoot captain, Pascal. He is tall, dark, and lanky with enormous splayed flat feet rimmed with caramel coloured cracked soles. Quick to smile, with broad, straight, blinding white teeth, he has big dark chocolate eyes that twinkle mischievously. Pascal's boat is a small crude wooden, blue and white skiff, with a low, head bonking half cabin. Pascal straddles the chasm between boat and dock and extends a ham-like hand to assist us boarding the bobbing vessel. We jam ourselves into the small, gasoline fumed space, with the rest of the passengers. The windshield is Plexiglas and it is severed by a giant crack which has been drilled its length on each side and then sutured with heavy fishing line, creating a Frankenstein scar. Underway, Pascal constantly adjusts the coughing 30 horsepower outboard motor with a wrench. No lifejackets, no oars, and no bail bucket are in sight.

Half an hour of bumpy travel has passed when Pascal eases the boat, in reverse, into a large gap in the face of a small island. The crevice opens up into an enormous cave, Swallows Cave, one hundred and fifty feet deep into the center of the earth. It is breathtaking. Stalactites drip from the ceiling and submerged stalagmites push up, from the cave floor, in crystalline water. Pascal scrambles onto a ledge with a short piece of pipe, he strikes a large rock hanging like a giant's proboscis, on the cave wall. 'Bell Rock' reverberates, a church bell, in this, nature's cathedral. We snorkel the fairytale cave chock-a-block with iridescent blue baitfish swirling up from the bottom in cyclonic balls. The iridescence from the fish reflects from the dark wall of the cave casting an eerie glow, and light reflecting from outside paints the sand at the bottom of the cave a soft baby blue. At the entrance, a ledge full of shimmering reef fish plunges straight down to the indigo depths. Outside the cave, a sudden downpour sends torrents of heavy droplets bouncing like popcorn on the surface, pelting our bare backs.

Back on the boat, we slowly and reluctantly exit Swallows Cave and chug our way to another small island. Pascal eases close and drops the anchor. He points to a deep blue underwater patch, the watery entrance to Mariner's Cave. The sea is rough outside of the cave so Pascal will stay with the boat to keep it safe. One of our companions on the boat, Susan, has been here before. However, she says the last time she was here, when she swam into the cave, a large Tongan helped by pushing her through. She convinces us the swim in is difficult, but do-able. Our Lonely Planet guidebook says, "The swim into Mariner's cave is like swimming under the hull of a boat." The book doesn't say how large a boat.

We all collect, treading water, near the submerged entrance, trying to muster some courage. After conferring, Susan decides that she and Bob will go first and the rest of us will follow two by two through the small opening. Bob and Susan look at each other, take deep breaths, and disappear into the island! It is unnerving seeing the two of them swallowed up by this lump of limestone. Now it is my turn, along with Susan's friend, Carol. I am nervous but my mind races. I know that I am as strong a swimmer as Bob and I rationalize that if he can do it, then I can do it. Carol swims down and tells me she can see the bottom of Bob and Susan's flippers, something for us to swim towards. I gulp a big breath of air, keeping my snorkel clenched between my teeth. The snorkel gives me the false sense that air is available. I swim down too deep. It is frightening swimming into the ebony darkness not knowing how far I have to go to get my next lungful of air. I begin involuntarily releasing the air through my snorkel, my lungs near bursting. Banging my head lightly on the roof of the swim-through, I am relieved when Bob grasps my wrist and pulls me safely through and to the surface. Spitting my snorkel out of my mouth, I exhale explosively and gulp air hungrily into my oxygen-deprived lungs.

Later, I am mesmerized by Bob's account.

"I took a deep breath and swam down into the darkness. I was running out of air and in a panic. The air was bubbling out of my mouth and I thought I was going to drown. I spun around, clawing at the limestone roof of the swim-through with my fingernails. It felt as if I were buried alive in a watery grave. Just when I was going to be forced to take my first breath of salty seawater, I popped to the surface, my lungs filling mercifully with moist cave air. I was alone for what felt like an eternity. Suddenly, Susan surfaced behind me, deeper into the cave, sporting a big silly grin on her face."

The cave is spectacular. With each wave surging against the island from the outside, the air inside the cave fills with a heavy blue foggy mist. The mist settles and recedes with each ebbing wave and then reforms seconds later. We cavort like children, giddy in the majesty.

The swim out of the cave is easy, 'towards the light', a rebirth of sorts from a limestone womb.

Bob, to this day, always begins the telling of this story with, "That was the day she tried to kill me."

CHAPTER 6

Thailand – Southeast Asia

An International Incident Narrowly Averted

January of 2004, Bob and I embark on our first journey to South East Asia. After a couple of nights in Bangkok, seeking adventure, we board a first class sleeper train heading north to the city of Chaing Mai.

Tonight we ride our first tuk-tuk (a three-wheeled motorized vehicle) to Thana Guest House for a six p.m. orientation meeting. We have booked a three-day 4x4 jeep trip with a guesthouse, which caters almost exclusively to Israelis. The meeting is interesting; Bob, I, and our guide are the only ones who speak no Hebrew. The only non-smokers in the room, we find ourselves trapped on a narrow hard wooden bench behind a table, while the smoky noisy mayhem surrounds us. "My God, what have we gotten ourselves into now?" I whisper apprehensively into Bob's ear.

A good-looking young man extends his hand in introduction, "My name is Tal, please excuse the behavior of my companions. We are really a nice bunch of close friends. Our country is at war and we are all somewhat stressed by the news we are hearing." Several of them huddle anxiously around a small television, listening to breaking news from home, car bombings, and people dead. Tal is around twenty-five, tall, athletically built, a soldier's body, with a confident, arrogant air. He has thick straight sandy hair, expertly coiffed, and large brown pools of melted chocolate for eyes, his features angular and chiseled. I envision him clad in a khaki jumpsuit, shiny polished leather boots, standing casually, arms folded across his chest, posing at the wing of a bomber. He welcomes us warmly with a rehearsed charm, easing our reservations about making the journey with this young and energetic group.

When we realize that day one of the tour involves a visit to the touristy snake farm and the elephant rides, we enquire about shifting our trip to a different itinerary. We have been to both just yesterday and we really did not want to repeat them. The lady owner of the guesthouse assures us, "You will love this trip," but then she says something puzzling. "Is it because they are Israelis that you want to change the trip?" Bob and I are not prejudiced people and we certainly have no preconceived feelings towards Israelis. Confused, we have no idea what she means by this comment.

Meeting concluded we leave Thana in a tuk-tuk heading to our dinner at the Riverside Restaurant. The Riverside is a pleasant open-air affair with tables on a boardwalk, at the water's edge. Mosquitoes from the brackish water buzz around our ankles.

I have my first frustrating experience, at the Riverside, with an Asian squat toilet. In a tiny windowless stall, I squat over the white porcelain receptacle. Washboard ridges edge the rim where you position your feet, one on either side of the hole. I learn, too late, that your feet have to be precisely positioned or you (well, I actually) will pee all over your shoes and the floor.

Nice. Now, when you are finished doing your business, there is no flush mechanism. In the corner is a low concrete tub filled from a tap, to overflowing. A plastic dipper bobs on top. You simply fill the dipper with water and slosh everything down the drain, a not so delightful part of the Southeast Asian cultural experience.

In the morning, we wait in eager anticipation on the sidewalk in front of our hotel for our eight a.m. pick up. Bim Bim, who will accompany us as one of the guides, transports us to Thana where we mill around in a mass of confusion awaiting our departure.

Thin dark haired Israeli girls lug bulging duffle bags down the steep wooden stairs from the dorm rooms of the guesthouse. Blow dryers and curling irons with tangled cords spill from open zippers. They chatter incessantly, in a language we cannot understand, eyeing us suspiciously.

Our convoy consists of eight jeeps, accommodating thirty guests and four guides. It takes considerable time to get underway. Thana allows its guests to drive a jeep if they wish, something Bob and I are happy to leave to the guide. Approximately forty-five minutes is spent in orientation. There is a palpable thrum of excitement, grins, and ground gears.

Finally, the jeeps are mobilized. Before we are even out of Chaing Mai, our Israeli companions are misbehaving. One of the vehicles races up to pass his buddy and they travel side by side along the busy highway yelling back and forth. Our guide, Jo Jo, tenses. He is worried about the enormous fine he will receive if the police see them. The jeep eventually slides back into place and Jo Jo breathes a sigh of relief.

We redo the touristy snake farm and elephant show and after lunch, we head for the hills. Our first stop is a jungle waterfall spilling from a high cliff into a chilly pool. After a teeth chattering dip, we are off again to a lovely national park with a steamy, bubbling hot spring. We walk down a pathway to six small cascading pools, where we immerse ourselves in the soothing warmth. Languishing in one of the pools, we enjoy a conversation with a young Israeli couple. Not friends with the rest of the group, they express their distaste for some of the behavior of our travelling companions.

Back in the jeep, we settle in for the two-hour drive to the village of Pai. About an hour into the drive, I see red flashing lights on the road ahead. Bob is dozing beside me, the sun settling on the horizon and the sky darkening. I think we are coming up on a traffic accident but soon realize it is a Police checkpoint. A crude wooden barricade blocks the road. Jo Jo approaches slowly. The two police nearest us sport the largest, scariest assault rifles I have ever seen. I am reminded of just where we are; a wakeup call. Jo Jo knows these men. He has been doing the trip for six years and passes through their checkpoint once a week. He tells them the number of jeeps and the number of people and we are unceremoniously waved through. Jo Jo explains that the purpose of the checkpoint is to attempt to stem the flow of drugs from Myanmar (Burma) to Thailand. We are only eighty kilometers from the Burmese border. After passing through, we continue on our journey to Pai.

Our accommodation for the first night is at the Hui Ing Resort and Garden. It is dark when we arrive and Jo Jo ensures we are the first to receive our room key, an obvious show of respect for our age. The cabins are cute clean little double units. We are exhausted. No sooner are our backpacks plopped onto the bed than the Israeli throng arrives. The noise, yelling, laughing and shouting, overwhelms us. With wide-eyed resignation, Bob and I realize that there will be no sleeping tonight.

After showering, we head to the restaurant for a late nine-thirty p.m. dinner. The cacophony continues. The Israelis perform a prayer ceremony in Hebrew using their paper napkins as yarmulkes - a ceremony, one of the girls explains which they do every Friday before their supper. We feel slightly uncomfortable and out of place, but we feel privileged to have the opportunity to experience their culture and religion.

At the conclusion of their ceremony, one of the more vocal women buzzes outside the kitchen yelling at the cooks, "We are all vegetarians I hope you know." Bob and I look sideways at each other and I speak up, "Excuse me, we are not vegetarians." We are totally ignored; it is like we don't even exist!

Steaming plates of food are placed on the table and a dogfight ensues. Near empty dishes are eventually passed our way. One of the cooks spots what is happening from the kitchen and she brings out a steaming heaping plate of stir-fried veggies and deposits it between Bob and me. When one of the girls reaches for it, she scolds her, "This is for them!"

At dinner, we realize that there are splinter groups in our troupe, eight or ten people who are not travelling with the main group. They obviously are not impressed with our travelling companions' behavior but they are Israeli and therefore, unwilling to form alliances with us. It is like a bad episode of the television show, 'Survivor'.

After dinner, Bob approaches Jo Jo and asks if there is any chance of us moving to a quieter room. He is a little reluctant at first but he finally agrees to relocate us to a small row building, perched on the river's edge, where the guides will be sleeping. We leave the others partying at the fire pit and Bim Bim escorts us to our serene little retreat. After enjoying a cold beer, we peacefully drift off to sleep, soothed by the trickle of the stream outside our door and lulled by the distant hum of the party gathered around a roaring bonfire.

The property we are on displays its true beauty in the light of day and it is a jewel consisting of many buildings and cabins spread over acres of land terraced down to the river. The landscaping is exquisite, dotted with deep red flowering poinsettias. Our room has a door opening onto a narrow tiny balcony overlooking the muddy reedy river.

The day is scheduled to start at nine-thirty a.m. Poor Jo Jo. These Israelis are almost unbearable. It is as if they are on their own agenda. When he says it is time to load up the jeeps and be on our way, they scatter. Shuffling restlessly alongside the guides, we are aghast at the lack of respect shown to the schedule, the guides, and to us. It is ten-fifteen a.m. before the jeeps are finally mobile.

Our first stop is Lod Caves; three caves connected by water during the rainy season. When full, Thai guides escort tourists on bamboo rafts from cave to cave but now, there is not enough water in the river for such a journey. Schools of large black carp boil in a shallow pool at the cave's entrance, competing for food thrown by the tourists as they cross a small bamboo bridge. Petite Thai women crouch in the entrance, waiting to light our way with large chrome plated gas lanterns. The cave is gorgeous but unfortunately without rules. Anything that can be reached has been touched. Bob and I have been into many properly preserved and protected caves over the years and it is heart-breaking to see people touching newly forming stalagmites and stalactites; sucking the life and breath out of this miraculous creation of nature. On the positive side, the local people are making a living from this natural resource. This without realizing that even the carbon dioxide given off by the gas lanterns is slowly killing their livelihood.

Lunch is Pad Thai, served to us buffet style on crude picnic tables set at the river's edge. After lunch, we travel about forty-five minutes before turning off the main road. Heading up the mountain, the road soon narrows and quickly turns into a deeply rutted single lane of hard packed red earth. Judging by the depth of the ruts, it must turn into an ochre quagmire during the monsoons. Fortunately, we are travelling with Jo Jo, in the lead jeep; a fine rusty dust envelops our Israeli entourage. After a short rest stop overlooking the Burmese border, we slowly bump our way into the Lisu village.

The Lisu are a hill tribe from Tibet. Jo Jo cannot speak their language. He tells us there are approximately three hundred and sixty people in the village. They have no schooling and are illiterate. There are no police and no hospital. The village is completely isolated. The Thai government provides a doctor who visits once a week as well as a 4 x 4 pickup truck to use in case of emergency.

Built on bamboo stilts, the homes in the village are neat and tidy. The walls are made of split bamboo panels about eight to ten inches wide and the roofs are thatched. The surrounding jungle has provided all of the necessary building materials. Fences are constructed from woven bamboo strips. The villagers are totally self-sufficient having chickens, pigs, and a few horses.

Short and squat in stature, the Lisu are beautiful people with rounded faces and dark almond shaped eyes. As the jeeps approach, small groups of thin barefoot children race behind us and stir up rusty puffs of dust. These tiny waifs know the jeeps; news of our arrival spreads fast. We stop at a corner where a small store edges the street. Jo Jo brings a giant tin of cream-filled vanilla cookies for the children. Lining up behind his jeep like dominoes, so close they are touching each other, the children are well behaved, quiet, and polite.

What happens next is nothing short of obscene. The Israelis pull up and all hell breaks loose. They tease the children with too few candies making them jump for them like trained dogs! Chaos ensues. Refusing to be a part of the melee, Bob and I stand at a distance, watching in disgust. Jo Jo is soon at our side letting us know he appreciates our concern and the respect we are showing. He hangs his head, his shoulders slumping in embarrassment and resignation.

A tiny, traditionally dressed woman catches my eye. She is four foot nothing. Her ebony hair hangs from the nape of her neck to her rump in a tight neat braid; dark almond eyes sparkle and glow serenely. She has

Lisu Woman with "Two"

two beautiful babies, one swaddled on her back, and one swaddled on her chest. The twins are about eight or nine months old. Tiny, black, box shaped caps with red trim and pink tassels adorn their heads. Their chubby cheeks have a shiny, cracked, rosy weathered sheen and their noses are crusted with snot. Waiting for the right moment, I approach slowly while the crowd throngs in the background. Holding out several ten baht coins and using charades, I ask permission to take her picture. Her eyes sparkle with a knowing light as she smiles. She points to her babies and simply says, "Two." I lamely attempt conversation babbling on, "I have twin grandbabies, and I know how hard your life is, caring for them." I think of my divorced daughter back home struggling in the western world with 'two'. She indulges my babbling, smiling serenely, not understanding a word of what I say. One of the Israeli girls notices our exchange and pushes her way in front of me. "Let me take a picture," she whines. "You can when I am finished!" I snarl. "She has two babies. Give her some money!"

Leaving the village, we bounce down the mountain to spend the night in a small town called Mae Hong-Son at the Baiyoke Chalet. It is a nice clean little hotel, in the center of town. Shortly after we are assigned our rooms, an Israeli battle ensues. A catfight erupts in the hallway between two of the girls from the room beside us. Bob and I attempt briefly to ignore it; perhaps it will run its course and be over with soon. No, that is not going to happen. We both go out two or three times to tell them enough is enough! Poor Jo Jo suddenly appears and vainly attempts a peace agreement, but it is a no go. Unbelievable!

Hours later, at dinner, the girls proffer a feeble apology. "Sorry for our behavior in the hallway earlier, we will try not to let it happen again." Bob blows a gasket, *"IT WILL NOT HAPPEN AGAIN! I WILL HAVE YOU SENT PACKING!"* Jo Jo sits at the head of the table; a smile briefly plays across his lips.

Our nine a.m. departure, the next morning, happens at nine-fifteen, better at least. Our destination today is the Karen longneck and Karen big-eared tribes. The troupe's behavior is slightly improved.

The longneck village is a deliberate tourist attraction. The tribe is far more accessible than the Lisu we visited yesterday. Buses of tourists arrive on day trips from the cities. The longneck women sell their souvenirs and wares from small lean-to stands. The tribe is healthier and wealthier.

The Karen tribes are originally from Myanmar (Burma). The women are beautiful, tall, slim, and fine featured, polar opposites of the Lisu. At five years old, the girls get the first of what will be many, shiny brass rings welded around their necks. As they grow, more and more rings are added, the more rings added, the more beautiful and desirable the girls are considered. These rings stretch and weaken the vertebrae in their necks to such an extent that if removed, their necks would be too weak to support the weight of their heads; a torturous consequence in the name of beauty.

Wandering the stalls, I purchase a souvenir from one of the women. She tucks the bills swiftly into the rings around her neck, a strange sort of lockbox.

I notice a baby, on a blanket, lying on a platform across from her mother's shop. I stand chatting to the baby, baby talk, eliciting easy smiles. Mom crosses the dusty lane and sits on the platform, hefting baby onto her lap. She is tall and slender with midnight eyes, milky skin, and a bright red lipstick smile. A regal air envelops her. The rings on

My New Longneck Friend

29

her neck widen under her jaw and at her collarbone creating a Midas' hourglass. Her short, ebony hair is tied back with a flowered bandana. Patting the boards of the platform, she says, "Come. Sit." " You speak excellent English," I marvel. "Did you learn it from the tourists?" "Yes," she replies. We sit and chat, just two women sharing an intimate moment. She tells me her baby is six months old, and her first child. She says there are one hundred and nine people in the longneck tribe, only twenty-six of them women. I ask if the rings are uncomfortable and she says, "No, you get used to them, they start putting them on when we are five." I ask, "Will your daughter get rings?" She replies a simple, "Yes." She enquires as to where I am from and when I say Canada she says, "You are a long way from home." When it is time for us to leave, she gently clasps my hand in friendship. Humbled, I tell her I am honored to have met her. Our exchange was so simple yet, so profound. I walk away carrying something of enormous value, 'Not For Sale' at a souvenir stand. I glimpsed the person behind the tourist attraction, a woman with dreams and desires, a woman who loves her husband and her baby, a woman on the other side of the world, and a woman not unlike me.

We leave the village and travel for about one and a half hours to our lunch stop. It is here at which the trip for poor Jo Jo goes from bad to disastrous.

We are uncertain just what is going on but the first sign of trouble is when Jo Jo comes over to the table where the Israelis are sitting and simply loses it. He says, "In the six years I have been doing this trek, you are the worst group I have ever had! You complain everywhere, about something, the rooms, the food, everything!" He stomps off, shaking his head in disgust. Up until now, he has maintained a steely patience. The Thai do not like conflict. Thais do not like arguments and see them as a loss of face. Soon after Jo Jo's tirade, we learn that a Jeep has gone missing with four Israelis and no guide. Jo Jo is distressed beyond belief. He paces back and forth, back and forth, hands on hips, head hung low.

Our next destination is river rafting and since we have done it before, we volunteer to remain behind, with Jo Jo, to await the lost Jeep. He sends the others on their way, sending one Jeep to search, while we wait at the lunch stop. Moments later, he receives a cell phone call from his office, his boss. The missing Jeep has called from the longneck village saying they have been left behind. There is now no possibility of a cover-up. His boss keeps saying, "Why Jo Jo? Why?" He is genuinely worried for his job and infuriated with the Israelis.

While we wait, Bob and I have a coffee and chat with a young Israeli couple in the restaurant. They are not part of our group. Sitting in the restaurant, as our group had their lunch, they were so appalled at the behavior that they waited to register at the small hotel, fearing the owners would think they were with us. They are visibly embarrassed. They ask where we are from and ask us if we understood what our Israeli companions were saying. When we say no we did not, they simply say, "Good." A delightful couple, we enjoy chatting with them. When we part they have a somber, *we really feel sorry for you*, look in their eyes.

The missing Jeep returns, escorted by the one sent to look for them. The occupants have the nerve to argue about having missed lunch. Jo Jo climbs into our Jeep, slams the door, and speeds off with us in the back seat, leaving two of our Israeli passengers standing in the parking lot after yelling at them, "You can go with your friends!"

We connect with the rest of the Jeeps just in time to float down the river on pole driven bamboo rafts. Our raft, over weighted with our overfed western bodies, flounders in the current. Thai children bathing along the riverbank laugh and point, chattering and giggling at our antics.

Later, back on the road, our distraught guide is still stewing. He stops to lock-in the hubs of the jeep, at the base of the highest mountain in Thailand. Doi Inthanon is almost 2600 meters in elevation. 'Doi' is the northern word for mountain.

A hairpin switchback road leads to the summit and we climb slowly in darkness. The jeeps are stopped at a police checkpoint. The power is out. Weak candles flicker in the buildings. Jo Jo reaches under the driver's seat and hands the guard a bottle of whiskey wrapped in a white plastic bag, allowing us swift passage, and the use of the darkened toilets.

We take a short rest here. Bob is quiet and sullen in the seat next to me. Eventually, he says to me, "You know all those times when you have said to yourself, *I wish I had?* I don't want this to be one of those times." Thinking, he slowly unfolds himself from the back seat. I feel anxious at his unusual anger, "Where are you going?" He responds, "I know exactly what I am going to do." He seeks out Tal, the young man who welcomed us at the pre-trip meeting. Tal is slouched in the back of a Jeep laughing with his friends. Bob commands, "Get out. I need to talk to you." Tal can see Bob is angry and visibly upset. Bob asks him to pass his message on to his friends. Tal attempts a feeble explanation to which Bob says, "Don't talk. Just shut up and listen." Bob tells him that their behavior has been terrible on the entire trip and Jo Jo risks losing his job because of them. They are an embarrassment to themselves and to their country. He says that if each and every one of them does not have a letter of apology on Jo Jos' boss's desk before the morning they are all scum! Then he asks Tal if he has thoroughly understood him. I am proud of Bob. When he returns to our jeep he is shaking and having difficulty speaking.

Upon returning to Thana Guest House that night, Tal approaches me to apologize. He knows he dare not approach Bob. I answer back, "It is not to us you owe the apology to but to Jo Jo," and turning brusquely on my heels, I strut away.

We did have an amazing trek that could not be spoilt by the obnoxious behavior of our travelling companions, and a story worth telling.

An international incident narrowly averted.

A Line Drawn in the Sand

Days later we are back in the south. We rise at six a.m. Today is a travel day. Our taxi arrives at six-forty five a.m. to take us to the pier at Nathon where we board a Sea Tran ferry to Donask. Bussing from Donask to Krabi, we arrive at the pier at twelve-thirty p.m. for our three p.m. departure.

The boat to Phi Phi is crowded. The planked wooden ferry slices heavily through the foamy waves. The old diesel dame has been painted over many times, white and blue. The wind is brisk and the seas sloppy. We sit on the open deck near a heap of luggage, with the smokers. Salty sea air thickens my hair into an unruly sticky mass. After a short one-hour trip, we arrive at a bustling dock. The boat bumps up against a freighter unloading crates of fresh food for the small tourist island, cushioned by old black tires that scuff the white hull. Two thick planks are thrown from deck to deck, one on the bow and one on the stern. People push to be the first to disembark. Bob and I know better than to rush, so we hang back. I cross the narrow gangplank carefully, dragging my wheeled suitcase across the deck of the freighter and gingerly climbing down onto the dock. Deck hands lift down my suitcase. Bob waits for the boat to clear, he has his suitcase and our huge heavy backpack filled with dive gear. We have pre-booked a room for the night and I search the crowd of hotel touts for someone holding an 'Andaman Beach Resort' sign. I tell our Thai host that Bob will be a few minutes coming. While we await Bob, two young girls approach. They ask the fellow from Andaman Beach if they have rooms available. "We are full," is his brusque reply. "No room, we are full," he repeats. "Why are you standing there with that sign then?" one of the girls admonishes. "We are full!" he barks rudely, "No room!" As they walk dejected up the dock, he leans towards me and whispers in a conspiratorial tone, "Israelis. No good." Bob struggles his way off the ferry and happily surrenders our heavy dive bag to the aluminum luggage cart.

There are no taxis on Phi Phi, no cars. The hotels use well built aluminum carts with rubber-tired bicycle wheels, pushed, pulled, and dragged through the soft sand. The roads are no more than wide pathways of red paving brick. The island is shaped like a lopsided "H"; a sandy, low-lying isthmus in the center connects the two pieces.

Trundling behind our host in the stifling heat, we pass small shops, bars, restaurants, and dive shops. Our Thai friend beep-beeps a bicycle horn at meandering tourists to clear the way for the wide cart. By the time we reach the Andaman Beach Resort, we are dripping with perspiration. The resort is adequate for the price we are paying, but less than we expected. We decide to stay for only one night and go in search of a better room tomorrow.

Awakening to a lazy day, after breakfast we walk the narrow streets to see what the island has to offer. There is not far to go. Most of the island's transportation is by long tail boat to the isolated resorts and pristine sandy beaches. After signing up for a dive at one of the local dive shops, we then go to peruse the wares in the ever-present 'Seven Eleven' store. It sits on a crossroads. Seven Elevens are everywhere in Thailand, and a heavenly place to visit. One of the few public places with air conditioning, narrow and crowded, tourists blissfully stand in line in the frigid aisles, patiently waiting their turn at the till while clutching icy cold Chang beer and Bacardi Breezers.

After a light lunch, with a book cracked, I deposit myself on a hard plastic lounge chair overlooking the bay. Bob sits briefly, but as is usual, he is restless. He has the brilliant idea that we should hire one of the long tail boats to take us across the bay. "Look, over there, there is a beautiful private white sandy beach. No one is on it," he says excitedly. "Let's get our snorkel gear and get the boat to drop us off for the afternoon." He strikes up a deal with a boat captain, 200 Baht return. We are smart enough to agree to pay him on our return, ensuring our pick-up.

We pack our snorkel gear and Bob buys two large cold Chang beers, stowing them in the bottom of our daypack. The captain slides the long tail up onto the sandy shore and we climb over the bow into the narrow launch.

Long tail boats are used all over Thailand as taxis and to transport goods. Crude plank boats with a pointed bow arching up out of the sea, they are brightly painted in primary colours. Long-shafted gas engines, with tiny eggbeater propellers that can be tipped above the surface of the water, power them. The engines have no neutral and the props spin madly spraying water each time the captain tips the shaft into the air. Muffler-less and extremely noisy, they sputter out noxious gassy clouds of fumes.

Talking above the din of the engine is impossible. The ride across the bay is short and our captain eases us onto the secluded sandy beach. A few boats are anchored just off the shore. One, a sailboat, has snorkelers, in orange life jackets, bobbing around it like corks.

Our captain speaks little English but he points up the beach and says, "Look, monkeys." After disembarking, we spread out our bamboo beach mat and plop our snorkel gear onto the sugary sand. I watch as a speedboat edges in, close to the monkeys, and the tourists on board toss bananas to them. Camera readied, like a National Geographic photographer, I stealthily approach. Bob hangs back worried he will spook them. The speedboat races off. One monkey at the water's edge turns over empty banana peels looking for missed tidbits. I cluck my tongue at him hoping he will turn for my photo as I snap a few shots, creeping

My Mini Mugger

ever closer. Looking up, I notice a pint-sized simian just above eye level on a tree branch, a baby. "Oh, I didn't see you sitting there, little guy," I coo, easing closer, not wanting to frighten him. I survey the scene through the camera lens, adjusting the zoom. All of a sudden, through the viewfinder, I see the baby monkey leaping from the tree branch directly at my camera! I am so startled; I fall flat onto my rump into the sun-warmed sand. Curling up into a ball, fetal position, I wail, *"BAAAAB!"* Mayhem ensues. Monkeys jump me from all directions. They pull at my camera strap, my purse strap, and my clothes. All I can think of is: *Please don't bite me! Please don't bite me!* Monkeys can carry rabies and a bite would mean a series of painful shots. Bob races up the beach swinging our daypack weighted with the two Chang beers, challenging my mini muggers. His feet sink into the soft sand slowing him. The monkeys scatter as I manage to stand up on shaky legs. Just as Bob reaches me, a big alpha male charges from under the tree line. Sand flies into the air at his abrupt halt, a line literally *'drawn in the sand'*. The big male's mouth stretches in a wide circle exposing pointed yellow fangs. A threatening guttural growl pierces the air. Bob stands his ground, and mimicking the territorial beast, he growls back, puffing out his chest in an attempt to look larger and more threatening. The large male primate hesitates briefly and then charges again, growling, fangs exposed. Bob growls back. Like gunfight opponents in a spaghetti western, they stare each other down. Eyes locked, slowly, we back away. Once we are at a safe distance we retreat to our beach mat, hearts pounding, and then we start to laugh. We laugh so hard tears dribble down our cheeks. Our faces flush red. Between burst of laughter, I tell Bob, "I am just grateful my Alpha male was bigger than their Alpha male." We howl with nervous laughter, gasping for breath.

Cracking one of the warming Changs, we toast the fact that I have escaped unscathed with no bites or scratches. As we watch, another tourist boat eases up to the beach tossing food. One of the tourists disembarks and one monkey gets aggressive and bites.

When the boat leaves, the monkeys start slowly and nonchalantly making their way up the beach towards us. They scare us. We have nothing to feed them and even if we did, they would only be satisfied until it was gone. To try to distance ourselves from them, we wade around a little rocky point. Quite small, the rising tide is threatening to swallow up the patch of beach altogether. Bob wades out chest deep in an attempt to keep an eye on the troupe's movements. It will be hours before our long tail taxi returns. Waving our arms, we try desperately and unsuccessfully, to get the attention of passing boats. A young couple in a kayak paddles close. We tell them of our harrowing adventure and ask if they can *PLEASE* paddle over to the sailboat and have the long tail boat along side of it come and rescue us.

The monkeys, watch amused. Relieved, we climb over the bow and into the safety of our rescue boat.

Manta of My Dreams

Scuba diving in Koh Tao and Koh Phi Phi is excellent but we keep hearing from dive masters, the Similan and Surin Islands off the coast, where Thailand borders Burma, is where the best diving is.

The dive masters and guides we meet are young and adventurous, oft times tattooed and pierced. Spirited souls, they love the lifestyle and the travelling the job affords them. They do not do the work for money; their wages are low and supplemented with tips from the divers. The places they live in are shared with other guides and dive masters. They are, after all, living in a tourist destination and the rent is not cheap. Far from home, in a job they love, they form bonds with each other, and often relationships leading to marriage. Marriages of mixed races are often performed without the presence of parents who would never understand and seldom give their blessings. We find invariably that we are the oldest divers on the boat and because of this, the guides look out for us, perhaps missing aging parents back home whom they haven't seen for months or even years.

Bob and I travel to Khao Lak. A Canadian couple we met previously on Koh Samui said it was a good place to visit; quiet, non-touristy, the type of place we seek out. Also, it just so happens to be a jumping off point for the live-aboard dive boats which travel out to the Similan and Surin Islands.

Khao Lak is a sleepy little fishing village about as far removed from the sleaze and glitter of Phuket as you can get. It has a few small resorts. Dive shops and thatched roofed restaurants line the beach. Tables with soiled tablecloths sit scattered unevenly in the sand. Fish, squid, and lobster, displayed fresh on a bed of ice, stare back with blank, milky, glazed eyes.

Bob and I walk the beach in search of a dive shop for our live-aboard excursion. A little uneasy about the diving, we have been told it is unforgettable but also challenging, with lots of current, meant for intermediate to advanced divers.

Eventually settling on a shop, the young lady reassures us we will be fine, "You can dive at your own level, whatever you are comfortable with. We will even give you your own dive master if need be."

A truck picks us up from our resort at six p.m. We stop briefly at the office to square up bills and to sign the waivers common to all dive operations. The, *'If you die, it's your fault, not ours'*, waivers. We climb into the back of an open truck, sitting on hard wooden benches facing each other. Our dive gear is piled high in the back of another small pickup truck. A heightened excitement buzzes as the group travels to the marina on winding potholed roads.

At the pier, relaying gear, we scramble over four dive boats to reach our launch, the Manta Queen. She is only four months old, but roughly built she looks much older. Our assigned cabin is roomy, with a double bed and deep drawers for stowage, underneath. The Manta Queen has a large open aft deck lined with dive tanks and three unisex combination washroom/showers. The galley is forward and a second level deck serves as the dining room where all of our meals will be served and where our dive briefings will take place.

Bob and I are the oldest, and the least experienced divers on board.

All aboard, the Manta Queen slowly chugs away from the dock. The night sky is inky and moonless. Still inside the harbour, the crew ties the boat up to a large orange mooring buoy. The boat bobs as the young Thai crew assembles on the bow near the Buddha point, a shrine decorated with dried flowers and incense to appease the gods. A crewmember opens a cardboard shoebox and extracts an enormous coil of red finger-size firecrackers. The coil is wound around a bamboo pole that is held by one of the deckhands. Another deckhand lights the fuse and the night sky erupts. The firecrackers spit sparks and red paper like a machine gun run amok. Gods appeased, we are now safe to continue our journey out of the harbour.

Dinner is served buffet style, simple but plentiful. That night the crossing is relatively smooth, however a sideways slop against the thin hull and the rumble of the diesel engines, along with the drone of the generator, make sleep impossible. Early morning, the crew wakes us to gear up, before breakfast, for our first dive in the Similan Islands.

Bob and I are provided with a private dive master, Chris. He and his young wife Katja are from Sweden. Katja is training to be a dive master and she will accompany us. The only other person diving with us is a forty something German fellow named Heinrich. Heinrich purports to be an experienced diver but he is what is known as an 'air hog' in dive circles. Out of air long before anyone else, the other groups are tired of him cutting their dive time short. The others are going deeper than us, increasing their air consumption, and Heinrich keeps forcing them to surface far too soon. Heinrich is a nuisance. He flails, kicking wildly with his fins threatening to dislodge your mask. He lands heavy on top of you and never stops to check to see if you are okay or to apologize. We also suspect Heinrich is drinking beer at lunch before dives, an absolute taboo.

The diving is breathtaking. Hawksbill turtles munch on bubble coral. An opalescent cuttlefish the size and shape of a football, hovers near the sandy bottom, finger like tentacles extending from its lumpy head; opaque side fins undulating. Rainbow colour bursts of reef fish paint the underwater canvas. Garden eels, pencil thin, stand like question marks, posed to retreat quickly into their sandy holes at the first sign of danger. Purple and cream anemones house orange and white clownfish, Nemos darting shyly in and out of their symbiotic hosts. Iridescent blue parrotfish crunch on coral with their hard beaks; the scratchy sound shatters the silence of the deep. White eyed and honeycomb moray eels poke their heads out of crevices, their sharp-toothed mouths opening and closing rhythmically with each breath. On one dive, we travel the length of a rusty shipwreck in a school of hundreds of porcupine puffer fish. Teardrop shaped, their melon sized heads taper to a pointed tail. Soft beige in colour with dark polka dot spikes and huge, round, bulging lidless eyes, they hang in suspended animation, eyeing us, amused. Chris lays his hand on a shelf in a niche of the wreck and striped cleaner shrimp approach, manicuring his cuticles.

Tonight we brave the night dive. It seems safe enough, quiet bay, and a mooring line to descend, but I am uneasy. I don't like night diving. I feel claustrophobic, enclosed in a dark water-filled grave with no way out.

Bob, Chris, Katja, and I enter the water last, swimming on the surface towards a large orange mooring buoy, fighting a brisk current. We descend the line in darkness and swim along the wall opposing the swift water. I notice a brilliant red crab in a sandy-bottomed boulder cave. My small dive light illuminates his stage, spotlighting his vaudeville act. I expect him to don a top hat, grab a cane, and do an old soft shoe for my entertainment. I giggle into my regulator. Continuing our swim, we notice the other groups have turned, passing us in the opposite direction. They wave cheerily, as the current sweeps them by.

Bob's flashlight quits and he fumbles in the pocket of his dive vest for his spare. Katja sees me struggling to help him find it and mistakenly thinks Bob is in distress. The light finally extracted, she realizes he is fine and gives him the *'You okay?'* signal. Turning, we drift back in the opposite direction, and in the fast moving water, we are soon back at the mooring line. Chris signals, "Do you want to go up, or go on?" Bob shrugs, looking questioningly at me. I am stressed, the current exacerbating my level of uneasiness. Only fifteen minutes into the dive, but I have had enough; I signal, I am ready to surface. Slowly we ascend the line to the buoy. The Manta Queen is a fair distance away and Chris signals with his flashlight for the Zodiac pick-up boat. Someone on deck of the Manta Queen acknowledges us with a flash back but no one is coming. Chris is annoyed at the lack of response and he suggests that we attempt drifting with the current towards the Manta Queen. Bob says, "No. We are all safe where we are. They will come." Suddenly, the Manta Queen starts up and leaves its mooring line. Left without a choice, we hang, suspended on the buoy, gazing up at a velvety indigo sky sprinkled with diamonds. We talk, sharing life stories. Chris frets, "No one is coming for us." We bob in the warm salty water. About thirty minutes later, the Manta Queen is back on the mooring buoy and relieved, we hear the dinghy heading our way. Hefting our gear over the side into the Zodiac, one by one we do a clumsy belly flop onto the deck; rescued at last. "What took you so long?" Chris chastises the Thai boy. "We waited so long, why!"

Back on board the Manta Queen, it quickly becomes apparent, why. Stories are buzzing. The groups were split apart; drifting in the swift current, they were swept out of the bay in darkness. Batteries dying, flashlights threaten to extinguish. Divers have nightmarish visions of frenzied sharks. Nerves are rattled. Smug, we secretly congratulate ourselves for our decision to surface at the safety of the mooring buoy.

We enjoy a cold beer on the deck as a giant blood-red full moon balloons on the horizon.

In the morning, Bob wakes with a killer migraine, or should I say, he has a migraine, which kept him awake most of the night.

He isn't fit for diving. Encouraging me to go without him, I hesitate, arguing lamely, but only briefly.

The first dive is at Koh Bon. There is some current, so Chris, Henrick and I, hang back from the crowd of divers. Chris pokes around the reef looking for interesting life. Distracted, I look over my left shoulder, towards the deep blue. Involuntarily, my heart pounds in my chest. I kick my fins a couple of times, grabbing Chris by the end of his fin, and shake. A four-meter manta is winging his way towards us. His black scooped cephalic lobes siphon in seawater, and as his wing tip dips, an uneven white saddle fades as it crosses a massive ebony back. His white underbelly is scored evenly by gill slits. Soaring gracefully, he is uplifted by the gentle ocean currents. Regal, at this moment in time, he owns the ocean. I stare skyward filled with wonder, awed and stilled. Sunrays pierce the surface creating an aura illuminating this giant of the deep. I hover humbly in his shadow sharing a spiritual moment with one of God's great creatures.

CHAPTER 7

Gibsons, BC - Canada

Tsunami

December 26th, 2004, I sit in the comfort of my living room watching news footage as a Tsunami sweeps over the west coast of Thailand. Two of the hardest hit areas are Koh Phi Phi and Khao Lak.

Shaky poor quality amateur videos from tourist cameras fill the news. I sob as a muddy wave washes over the pool at the hotel where we stayed on Phi Phi, leaving the mushroom shaped fountain in its center askew. Footage shows Christmas vacationers frolicking on beaches unaware of the danger thundering towards them. Background voices on the videos are near hysteria as they yell in vain from their balcony vantage points hoping to warn the people dotting the beaches. An older, balding man, clings in the maelstrom to a palm tree as plastic deck chairs speed by him in the raging water.

That day, the news stations re-run the clips repeatedly and each time as I watch in stunned silence, I am hopeful that the outcome will be different. Tears spill from my eyes and stream down my cheeks.

In the evenings, when Bob and I were on Phi Phi, we would walk the narrow sandy isthmus between Loh Dalum Bay and Ton Sai Bay. Sitting at a little seaside bar, feeling like illicit lovers, we would enjoy a dewy glass of cold white wine. The waitress, having gotten to know us, would bring us our refreshments without asking us our pleasure. As the sun was setting, we would watch, as Para-gliders were lifted off the sand, high into the air, by brightly coloured nylon kites.

The water recedes from both of these bays just before the tsunami hits. The tsunami strikes from both sides colliding in the middle of the narrow isthmus. The island is devastated. Over seventy percent of its buildings are destroyed. Debris is everywhere, boats high and dry, palm trees crisscrossed like match sticks; stiff limbs poke out, bodies buried under the rubble. Dive boats slowly return to the island, unaware of the devastation that has occurred on land. The Thai government declares the island temporarily closed.

Stories of miracles slowly emerged. Fisherman rescue strangers struggling in the churning maelstrom. It is no longer tourists and locals but a frantic jumbled mess of humanity. Families are separated. Loved ones are lost, gone forever.

The Thai government sends in ships and helicopters evacuating passport-less dazed tourists from the worse hit areas. Panicked foreigners trying to arrange flights home overwhelm the airports. Canvas tents spring up acting as triage centers, first aid stations, and makeshift morgues. Bodies are stacked uncovered, stiff like cordwood. The phone lines are down, making communication in or out of the country virtually impossible. Searching for friends and family, people wander the streets zombie-like viewing pictures posted on roadside bulletin boards of the dead and injured.

Approximately a month after the Tsunami, I receive an email from Katja. "Just making sure you are safe at home, and that you and Bob were not in Thailand at Christmas. Chris and I are safe at home in Sweden. I am taking a nursing course. I have heard news from Khao Lak. Everyone from the dive operation has miraculously survived."

You will be an awesome nurse, Katja. Bob and I will never forget you and Chris.

CHAPTER 8

Peru – South America

Mi Dios! Magical Mystical Perú

It is January of 2005 and we have no intention of going to Peru. Our destination this year is the Galapagos Islands but as fate would have it, we have enough airline points to get to South America and Air Canada has just added a new route to Lima. They do not fly into Ecuador. It is an opportunity we cannot pass up.

We book a two-week tour with GAP Adventures; the first of many times we will use GAP, a Canadian based company launched in 1990. Their founder, Bruce Poon Tip, was a backpacker who wisely sensed a need for small group, budget, adventure travel, and is a true Canadian success story.

Arriving safely in Lima, we take a taxi to our hotel. The Antigua in Mira Flores is an old Peruvian mansion without an elevator. Three floors are horseshoed around a small courtyard blooming with fragrant tropical flowers. A cement pond filled with slimy green stagnant water sits in the center. We are on the third floor. The rooms are large with a television set, bar fridge and huge, tiled, full bath. The hotel, including our room, is filled with gorgeous, if somewhat worn, antiques. The bases of the tables in the small restaurant are all old treadle Singer sewing machines and all of the lamps are constructed from odd antiques. The lamp on the desk in our room is made from an old box camera with an extended accordion lens.

We are lounging on our penthouse deck when our phone rings. It is Luis, our tour leader. "Most of the guests are having a drink in the lobby. Do you want to join us and go for dinner?" The majority of our group has arrived but a few will arrive in the morning so our orientation is delayed until then. So far our group consists of two Canadians, Barb, a human resources worker from Hamilton, Ontario, Brian, a lawyer, also from Hamilton; Brandon, a young good old boy from Texas, Karen and Tim a young couple from Tasmania, Australia, and Alan, an Englishman from Cornwall who is the oldest in our group. Our group leader, Luis, lives in Venezuela with a sister and his young daughter from a failed marriage.

Luis is a complex character who has lived an amazing life of adventure. In his younger days, he spent time scuba diving in the rivers of Venezuela, mining gold. He would partner up with his brother, whom he trusted to man the compressor, which was his air supply up on the raft. There were untold numbers of stories of divers drowning when the compressor ran out of gas as the attendant dozed. The divers, submerged in the muddy water wearing old-fashioned brass diving helmets and weighted boots, carried a four-inch suction hose under their arm. They sucked the mucky earth from the river bottom up to the raft to be processed. It was extremely dangerous work but at the age of nineteen, Luis was able to afford a motorcycle in a country where much of the population goes to bed hungry. He was young, on top of the world and invincible. When he was older, Luis worked in the *Special Police* forces. He enthralls us as he tells a tale of getting shot in the back. He lifts up his shirt to show us a deep depression just below his shoulder blade into which a thumb could easily fit. He tells us about government corruption and a time when they were sent on a covert mission to assassinate a presidential opponent.

Luis, guiding us on our Peruvian adventure, could prove exciting indeed.

Luis escorts us on foot to a large outdoor restaurant set up on a closed off section of the street near Kennedy Parque. The food is excellent. I order a traditional Peruvian dish called Taku Taku, which is seafood cooked in a mild Creole sauce and then poured over a mixture of rice and beans. Some of the braver amongst us order a more radical fare. Brian orders the alpaca and he insists we all taste it. Tim nails it when he describes it as the taste of kidney, a slightly dry gamey taste. Brandon, the Texan, orders cuy, which is guinea pig. Peruvians raise guinea pigs in cages, for food. The animal is killed, gutted, and stripped of its skin. The cook then butterflies flat the entire body, including the head, using strong bamboo skewers. The Cuy is either grilled over hot coals or dipped in flour and deep-fried until crispy. The taste elicits the old standard, 'tastes like chicken'.

At our orientation in the morning, we meet the rest of our group: two young girls from Melbourne, Australia, and a doctor from New York, Sheila. After our orientation, we return to our rooms to pack. The bus picks us up at twelve-thirty p.m. and we are off on a wild and crazy ride to the airport. Horns honk, cars careen through intersections and there are near misses as cars squeeze through impossibly narrow spaces. A fire truck, sirens blazing, tries unsuccessfully to gain headway. The traffic takes no notice as, over a loudspeaker, the fireman barks orders to clear the road. We sit stalled in the melee, slowly inching our way towards the next leg of our journey.

Finally, at the airport, we are now sitting on our Lan Peru flight, waiting, waiting, and waiting. We are not sure why. I overhear a stewardess say in English, "There is no reason for concern." "What? Bob, did you hear that?" " What? What? No." The stewardess comes around with a tray of juice and I chuckle when Bob chooses a neon lime-yellow glass of Inca Cola. A popular refreshment in Peru, it looks like antifreeze, smells like Bubble Gum and tastes like a thick sickeningly sweet Cream Soda. The captain updates us on our flight status; we are waiting for a tire to be changed on the landing gear!

Before we left the hotel today, as a precaution, we decided to take the medication we had brought along for altitude sickness. We are flying to Puno, the highest destination on our trip at 3800 meters above sea level. As we waited for our bus at the hotel, I asked, "Bob, are you feeling okay?" "Yes, why are you asking?" "I feel funny, my feet are tingling, and I feel a little off." "Yeah, I am feeling a little strange also, now you mention it." The tingling seems to move from my feet to my fingers to the roof of my mouth to my face. Perhaps it would have been better to brave the altitude sickness. Now we are sitting on the plane, four hours later, and what a buzz. I keep brushing imaginary hair away from my face and if I touch my face the tingling stops briefly and then radiates out from my fingertip in circles like when a rock is dropped into a glassy pond, freaky. I feel like I am on a weird acid trip.

Our plane is finally off the ground and a quick one-hour flight takes us to Cusco and then on to Juliaca, twenty-five minutes away. As we are exiting the plane, I notice a small red warning sign emblazoned on the door of one of the overhead compartments. The sign reads, '*Jungle Survival Kit*'. I point it out to Tim, our tall, bald Tasmanian companion, who is walking up the aisle behind me, and he quips, "It is probably just knives and forks, and salt and pepper." I snicker uncomfortably, knowing he is alluding to the story of the Uruguayan rugby team stranded in the Andes after a plane crash, and forced to resort to cannibalism to survive.

Peruvian music fills the airport at Juliaca. As we wait for our luggage, pan flutes, drums, and odd percussion shakers made from the toenails of alpacas serenade us. A forty-five minute bus trip takes us to the Pukara Hotel in Puno. Our room is on the third floor and schlepping our luggage up the stairs is a monumental feat. We are all huffing and puffing from lack of oxygen and I overhear some of the youngest of our group questioning their decision to do the Inca Trail.

Puno is surreal, a trip back in time. The streets are narrow and potholed. Adobe fences surround homes and three wheeled pedal bike taxis bounce by, looking for fares. Tiny, poorly lit shops are crammed with wares. Cheap neon signs light their doorways. The natives are striking in their traditional, woven cotton clothes. Sturdy folk of small stature, dark skinned, brown eyed with glossy raven hair. Some of the older women wear tresses, in long tight braids, trailing down their backs to ample rumps.

In the morning, we are transported to the port on Lake Titicaca in three wheel bicycle taxis called cholo. Our drivers careen through the intersecting streets overtaking each other in a mad race. We laugh as they jeer and tease one another and marvel at their energy when we had difficulty scaling the flight of stairs at our hotel.

At the dock, we are met by an aluminum launch similar to a Canadian west coast water taxi. After shopping at the small dockside shops for water and gifts for our home-stay families, we board the boat.

Our first stop is Uros Island. Uros is a floating island made entirely out of totora reeds. The reeds are thick and shiny green with a white spongy centre when they are harvested, but dry into a strong straw like substance. Along the edge of the island is a wide, log-shaped bumper of reeds lashed together with rope. Top reeds are constantly replaced as the underbelly of

Uros Island – Lake Titicaca

the island slowly rots away. Stepping onto the island is like stepping onto a soggy sponge. The huts and teepee shaped homes of the small community are also constructed from totora reeds. Women cook lake fish and tiny birds in flame blackened cast iron pots and earthenware bowls over carefully tended fires. An uncontrolled fire would be like igniting a haystack. Scruffy children in hand-knit sweaters and tasseled hats tumble over thick reed logs that serve as benches. The children seem healthy, with the exception of runny noses and sores refusing to heal in the constantly damp environment.

After visiting with the villagers, we are transported on a mythical journey in a boat from an ancient fairy tale. The boat, long and low to the water, is constructed entirely from tightly lashed together totora reeds and silently manually propelled by poles at the stern. At the bow, a menacing two-headed dragon rises up out of the lake. I sit on the spongy deck spellbound, reflecting on the life that has brought me to this strange land.

Two Headed Dragon – Boat of Totora reeds – Uros Island

Reluctantly pulled back to present time, heady from our fairy tale adventure, we re-board our modern aluminum craft for the trip to Amantani Island and our home stay.

Lake Titicaca is enormous. Azure blue and dotted with tiny islands, if you didn't know better you would swear you were on the ocean. Deposited on Amantani Island, we sit on tiered rock benches patiently awaiting our assignments to our 'mothers', for the upcoming night. I study a single sheet of paper with some Quechua phrases, '*Maypitaj Wanu*, 'where is the toilet?'

Our 'mother' is Nellie. She wears traditional Quechua dress; a white blouse ablaze with embroidered flowers, a pleated, heavy, green wool skirt, and an intricately stitched sash, tied tightly around her thick waist. Her face is soft and round, young looking.

Nellie charges off ahead of us at a demanding pace, up the steep rocky pathway. Our 'home' is adobe brick; our room, on the second floor, is up steep, sloped, uneven concrete steps. A partial guardrail of jagged pipe in front of our blue and white door, fails to guard. We have to duck to enter the tiny portal. The room is bright and airy with lots of windows, three beds, and a kitchen table with three mismatched chairs. A bank of batteries sits in the corner, powering a bare energy saving fluorescent bulb screwed into a porcelain lamp holder on the low ceiling. Small red plastic potties are inverted under each bed. The alternate bathroom facilities, identical at every home, are government built outhouses. Sided in bright orange tin with a seat-less standard toilet, a full bucket of water sits outside for flushing.

We proffer our gifts of rice, sugar, and candles to Nellie along with some small gifts for the children, matchbox cars, and barrettes. Nellie is the most delighted with sparkly body stickers bought at the dollar store back home. She escorts us downstairs presenting us woolen hand-knitted hats with tassels and earflaps. Luis tells us later, the men do the knitting and the women can identify their charges by the hats they are wearing.

After settling into our room, we head downstairs to help prepare dinner. The kitchen is approximately fourteen feet by six feet. The walls, crudely plastered with red adobe mud, support several narrow shelves holding only the bare necessities of a kitchen. A couple of graters hang on nails and at the fireplace hangs a large, well used, cast iron fry pan. Grandma is in charge of the cooking. She sits to the right of the fire, propped on what looks like a stuffed sack. A stack of gnarled eucalyptus sticks sits at her side. She feeds them into a hot open fire that vents through a brick chimney. Additional eucalyptus branches are neatly stacked in the open rafters until required. A steaming cauldron stews and bubbles on a cast iron platform. The floor is hard compact dirt. Grandma constantly stokes the fire, flipping back her long greying braids, and gathering up her billowing purple skirt in an attempt to keep them out of reach of the licking flames. We peel tiny purple potatoes, with a small sharp paring knife, to add to the pot. I ponder that I would give anything to have a potato peeler in my backpack! The potatoes are small, their growth stunted by the lack of oxygen in the air. Dinner is watery potato soup with a few added vegetables, an unchanging meal each and every day.

Wearing Traditional Dress and our 'House Hats'

Following dinner, Nellie comes up to our room to prepare us for a dance at the community hall. She dresses Bob in a heavy brown wool poncho with stitched trim. His house hat completes the ensemble and he looks downright smashing. Nellie's costume for me is a little more elaborate. First, she pulls a beautiful cotton embroidered blouse over my head and then follows with a double layer of skirts. The under skirt is bright orange wool with yellow islet trim and the overskirt is pink, pleated and shorter. She then wraps an eight-inch wide brightly woven sash high around my middle, trussing it up just beneath my breasts. The combination of my carbohydrate filled dinner and a lack of oxygen, leaves me feeling faint and breathless.

"Vamos," says Nellie. Trundling behind her, we begin our onerous journey up the steep pathway to the community centre.

The dancing is lively, accompanied by drums, pan flutes, and alpaca toe shakers. As we enter the hall, we are simultaneously grabbed by festively dressed women and clasping hands in a circle, dance a long ten-minute jig that speeds to a dizzying finale. The rest of the night we beg off and watch as the younger crowd spins and twirls. The *chicas* flirt unabashed with Tassie Tim and Texas Brandon. One particular dance, Tim allows himself to be whipped around in a circle for a full fifteen minutes. As he passes us, he yells, "Help me!" or "Get me out of here!" The flaps and tassels of his house hat flip back and forth on his baldpate and his heavy poncho sways to and fro to the beat.

At daybreak, we hike up the pastoral mountain to a small open-air temple, to witness *'La Fiesta de San Sebastian'*. This festival is held once a year to bestow offerings to *'Pachamama'* or Mother Earth and to pray for a plentiful harvest. The temple is a circular rock wall approximately six feet tall. Inside are terraced stone benches. We edge our way to the far side of the temple and climb to the top for a good vantage point. Musicians from each village parade a labyrinth of worn pathways to the tempo of drums and pan flutes. They funnel into the temple, maneuvering their way to the stone benches. One of the band members then climbs to the top of the mortar-less rock wall planting several colourful flags. On a blanket, in a grassy patch, women in multi-hued garb deposit offerings of corn, potatoes, and bottles of thick, lumpy, yellow fermented corn beer. Bottles of the brew are saved and passed back and forth between the men, their instruments now resting in their laps.

During all of the activity, the Shaman is preparing the most sacred of offerings, one he had to travel to Puno to acquire. The Shaman spreads out a square of soft gauzy snow-white alpaca wool beside the other offerings and reverently lays down a brown shriveled form. Offering complete, the llama fetus is in place. We watch in awe, privileged to be witness to the sacred service. *(For information on this offering watch: 'Discovery Channel Videos: Solving History with Olly Steeds: Shaman Gift Shopping')*

Back down in the village we pack up our belongings and bid a tearful farewell to our host families. It is amazing how attached you become in such a short period. I sadly reflect on the fact I shall never again cross paths with people whom have touched my life in such a profound way, people who serve as building blocks to fortify my character.

Fiesta de San Sebastian – Shaman in the Foreground

The captain of the boat hurries our departure. A storm is brewing on the horizon. Dark grey billowing clouds are moving quickly across the expanse of the lake. As soon as we leave the dock, the water starts to bump up with white caps. Bob and I are boaters and we know the sturdy aluminum vessel can handle whatever the storm throws our way, however, the others are not at ease, and an edgy nervousness permeates the air. Big, strapping, Aussie Tim is pacing back and forth at the stern of the boat like a caged animal, "This is bullshit! We are going down! I want out of here!" Trying to act as a calming influence, Bob tells everyone we will be fine, and suggests we all don lifejackets and sit low in the hull of the boat. Our intrepid leader Luis chatters in Spanish with the captain. Waves wash over the bow obscuring the windshield. The captain, unable to see, dashes in a panic to steer the boat at the stern. He trips over his life jacket clad passengers.

An hour out the lake suddenly calms and the group relaxes, conjuring up tales in their heads of their harrowing journey, in a storm, on Lake Titicaca.

Safely back at the hotel, Luis tells us he was trying to convince the captain to beach the boat. He was terrified. "I was so *scaret*," he moaned. "I was saying my prayers and making my peace with God. I thought I would never see my daughter again!"

The captain argued that going closer to shore would cause us to capsize, and we should all surely perish. Thankfully, we had a knowledgeable captain at the helm today that saw us safely back to port.

Machu Picchu – Breath of the Incan Gods

Sheila, the doctor from New York, was bedridden for her entire time on Amantani Island. Faint and vomiting she suffered altitude sickness from the moment we arrived in Puno. Sheila planned on trekking the Inca trail but three days after arriving in Peru, she was forced to fly home.

My one regret on the trip to Peru is that we opted out of doing the four-day trek of the Inca trail. Bob and I are the only ones in the group left behind and it is extremely tough and emotional. We decided against doing the trail because of a combination of age and an uncertainty as to how each of us would handle altitude. In hindsight, we realize we would have fared well.

In September of 2007, two and a half years later, Bob and I complete the grueling 76-kilometer 'West Coast Trail' on Vancouver Island. Conquering the 'West Coast Trail', I thought of 'Machu Picchu', and the regret I felt for opting out of the Inca Trail evaporated from my soul.

A bus ride takes us from Cusco to Ollantaytambo where the group spends one night acclimating to the altitude before beginning their trek. Bob and I stroll the narrow cobblestone streets with them as they buy gnarled walking sticks and bags of green coco leaves to chew to ease altitude sickness. Later, we all have a beer in a sidewalk bar and watch as a glowing sun sets over the Andes.

The following morning, with the rising sun, we board the bus to take us to the trailhead at kilometer 82. The moment is bittersweet as Bob and I pose with the group for pictures. Tears flow as we hug them and say our goodbyes. Bob and I will spend the next several days in Cusco in comfortable beds while the rest of the group hikes the steep rocky trail carrying daypacks. Porters will run ahead on muscled legs wearing sandals made from recycled tires, carrying one hundred pound packs laden with the bulk

Incan Walls of Cusco – A single piece of paper will not fit between the mortar-less cracks!

of the supplies as well as the tents, food, and kitchens.

Days later in Cusco, we rise at five a.m. After breakfast, we take a taxi to the train station to catch a six-fifteen train to Aguas Calientes. The train chugs slowly out of the station but before it gains any momentum, it stops to chug in reverse. This grinding beast, its' cars clanking hard against each other, does a zig-zag, *forward-reverse-forward-reverse-forward-reverse*, each time zigzagging us up in elevation high above Cusco. Eventually, we start our forward journey. Gaining momentum, the train rocks gently side to side as it *click-clacks* towards Aguas Calientes. This tiny rail town has no cars. Buses await tourists arriving by train to take them to the entrance gates of Machu Picchu. Haphazard, roughshod construction, the buildings are brick, mortar, and wood, with corrugated tin or plastic roofs. It occurs to me, we are in the shadows of one of the architectural '*Wonders of the Ancient World*', construction so precise it is unfathomable and I snicker as I think what thoughts would run through the mind of an Incan worker if he were to walk these streets today.

Machu Picchu, scholars claim, was built around 1450 AD. In the 1500's, the Spanish Conquistadors systematically destroyed the Incan Empire, pillaging, stealing gold and riches, slaughtering the masses, taking prisoners as slaves, and decimating cities. Its obscure location miraculously spared Machu Picchu. Hiram Bingham discovered the ruins on a small expedition sponsored by Yale University and National Geographic. He brought the site to the attention of the western world in 1911.

Machu Picchu was completely self-sufficient with enough arable terraced land to feed its population. The site served as an important astronomical observatory, having an *Intihuatana* stone, a 'hitching post to the sun'. The stone, precisely placed, shows no shadow when the sun sits directly over it at midday, on March 21st and September 21st, marking the exact date and time of the two equinoxes.

The architecture is amazing and it is unclear how the Incas managed to move the enormous blocks, some weighing over fifty tons. Carved multi-faceted with such precision, it is impossible to slip even a single sheet of paper into the mortar-less cracks. Each block matches its counterpart so precisely that laser cutters today would find it difficult to achieve.

We rise early catching the bus from Aguas Calientes to Machu Picchu to reunite with our group. Tires riding precariously close to the cliffs' edge, the bus zigzags its way up the mountain on a dusty, single lane, switchback road.

At the entrance, we unload with the rest of the tourists. I feel as if I am waiting for my children to arrive home after a long journey. High up the mountain, the groups of hikers cross the top of the ridge on their final approach to the ruins. An hour and a half later, Brandon is the first of our group through the gate the others following close behind. We hoot and wave as each familiar face appears. They are exhausted, walking dead. Barb is on the verge of tears; Alicia and Lauren have had stomach problems. They are all bursting with stories of the challenging and grueling trail. Horizontal rain turned the trail into a stream on the second day and the nights were frigid. At different times, both Karen and Barb were brought to tears.

They are famished and dirty, with greasy stringy hair and a dank feral odor. Karen has dandruff the size of cornflakes peeling from the burnt part in her hair. Dragging heavy feet, none of them are able to take solid steps, even on level ground.

In an email she sent to her Mother, Karen said that the trail was the most challenging thing she had done in her entire twenty-nine years of life. *Karen along with Tim served in the Australian army reserve in East Timor. Terrified, she patrolled the town carrying an army issued rifle, wearing army fatigues and combat boots!*

The ruins and the surrounding mountains are shrouded in mist, which clears briefly and then reappears even thicker. I am desperately worried that we travelled all of this way to see nothing. Just as we enter the gates, the breath of the Incan Gods blows the mist away. We tour the ruins with our ragtag group, as they shuffle listlessly, too tired to enjoy the ruins they toiled so hard to see.

At the conclusion of the tour, Bob and I decide to climb Huayna Picchu, *'Young Peak'*; Machu Picchu meaning *'Old Peak'*. The climb is challenging and strenuous. The day has heated up. The stone stairs are steep and uneven and often we have

At Machu Picchu – Huayna Picchu is in the Background

to pull ourselves up with ropes and cables that are pinned into the face of the rock cliff. To allow opposing traffic to pass on the narrow pathway, we have to paste our bodies flat against the rock face. The climb is worth the risk. From our mountaintop aerie we look down into the valley upon a magnificent site, Machu Picchu laid out beneath us in its entirety. Heady with lack of oxygen we sit silent, mesmerized by the glory below us.

I have never before felt closer to God.

The Chakana

The Chakana is a powerful enduring symbol of the Inca civilization. Derived from the Quecha word 'chakay', it means 'bridge or portal'. The center of the cross represents the city of Cuzco, the capital of the Inca Empire, and the steps of the cross represent:

Work for:

Own Benefit   Upper World
Community   Current World
Government   After Life World

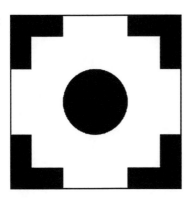

Love   Snake (Past)
Work   Puma (Present)
Knowledge   Condor (Future)

CHAPTER 9

Ecuador – South America

Darwin's Galapagos Islands

We spend the day in Quito, Ecuador going from travel agent to travel agent, pricing live-aboard boat trips. This is virtually the only way you can see the Galapagos Islands as the Ecuadorian government keeps a tight rein on the number of tourists allowed to visit at one time. Boats are on a tight agenda and must wait for other boats to clear the small islands before being allowed to take their passengers ashore. We book a seven-day excursion on a boat called the Sea Man at a cost of $850 American dollars each. In addition, we have to each buy a park permit for $100 American dollars and pay for the flight to the islands.

The Galapagos Islands are magical. Their geography keeps them isolated from contamination and they are known for their vast number of endemic species. In 1835, Charles Darwin arrived aboard the HMS Beagle to study the flora and fauna of the islands. The creatures here were instrumental in his developing the 'Theory of Evolution'. The islands lie approximately 972 kilometers off the west coast of Ecuador, and consist of thirteen large islands and six small islands with only five inhabited.

Aboard the Sea Man, we visit several of the uninhabited islands. An inflatable Zodiac ferries us to the small landings. The animals impress us with their lack of fear. A small bird lands on Bob's arm wanting the fresh water in his bottle; sea lions bask on the beach as a mother nurses an oversized pup. Walking rocky lava trails we come face to face with every sea bird imaginable. Nests are filled with white downy booby chicks waiting for their parents to return with food. Land iguanas bask on sun-warmed rocks in the pathways; some of the males challenge each other, others mate in pairs unabashed. Our guide, Mauricio, tells us the male marine iguanas have two penises but they use only one at a time. Lucky girls! Black frigate birds soar overhead, their bright red, balloon-like throats puffed out to impress the ladies. Others, perched in the trees, puff their necks to near bursting. Bobbing their heads up and down, they thump their beaks against the distended pouch producing a deep resonating drum beat sound. Orange and purple Sally Lightfoot crabs scamper over the rocks at the sea edge; marine iguanas swim swiftly through the surf munching on dark green seaweed; an enormous school of golden rays swim in the shallows and circling amongst them, is a school of two meter long Galapagos sharks. A golden owl rips apart a fresh kill as he eyes us suspiciously.

Another day we laugh, as we watch the 'dance of the blue footed boobies'. The mating pair squares off in an elaborate comical dance. The male has a shrill whistle and both of them hold their tails high in the air. Wings spread, they click-click-click their beaks like swordsmen fencing, and alternately lift their blue webbed cartoon-like feet.

Watch Out for the Beach Master

After an all night cruise, we awake in our morning anchorage, outside of Black Turtle Cove, rising early for a pre-breakfast dinghy ride. The cove is large, and Mauricio, wants us in at low tide. A maximum of two meters deep, the sandy-bottomed cove is ringed with mangrove trees, sitting high on their exposed root systems. The cove is the mating grounds for the black turtle, sub-species of the common green sea turtle. Voyeurs, we watch several mating pairs, the male riding on the back of the female, his penis tucked under her carapace to impregnate her clutch of eggs. Circling the large cove slowly, the guide shuts off the outboard engine silently paddling the Zodiac. We see spotted eagle rays skimming the surface and as the guide maneuvers the dinghy into a tidal stream, a school of one meter long white tipped sharks surf through the current, feeding on small fish. Pelicans, wings folded tight, dive awkwardly headfirst into the sea, filling their pouches with breakfast. Blue-footed boobies bask in the morning sunshine, preening.

After breakfast, the Sea Man anchors between North Plaza and South Plaza Islands. The plan is to snorkel before lunch. Bob has his underwater camera and we are pumped about the prospect of swimming in a school of sea lions. Mauricio cautions, "It is okay to swim with the pups and the females. Just be wary of the Beach Master."

A young Dutch woman, named Anika, asks if she can join us. Bob and I suit up in our short neoprene wet suits; tiny Anika is clad in a skimpy bikini. We swim excitedly towards the beach, circumnavigating a small rocky pinnacle near shore. The female sea lions circle Bob. One swims so closely underneath me I have to flatten myself on the surface to let her pass. The females, sensing Bob is the male, dive and cavort flirtatiously, as he spins around in an attempt to distance himself enough to take a picture. One

One of the 'Beach Master's' Harem

sea lion touches her nose to his camera lens. We are all laughing at their antics when, a giant silver behemoth glides past Bob. "Oh, no!" says Bob. "Was it a big one?" asks an alarmed Anika. "Yes!" responds Bob. I keep my masked face submerged in the water to keep track of the enormous bulbous-headed beast. As his adulterous harem scatters, I watch in horror as he glides like a spinning grey torpedo past Anika, circling around behind her. Opening his jaws wide, exposing huge triangular shaped teeth, bubbles escaping from his whiskered nostrils, he clamps down firmly on Anika's bikini clad butt cheek. Bob is looking directly at Anika. Her face fills with fear, and her eyes widen as she cries out, "He *BIT ME!*" Bob panics, uncertain how badly injured she is. Has she lost a leg? Bob whistles loudly through his fingers to get the attention of someone on the boat. Anika swims as quickly as she can away from shore and towards the Sea Man. A crewmember noticing our distress, heads out to rescue us in the Zodiac. I watched as the bite happened so I know Anika is not badly injured and as we swim, I try to reassure her that "The 'Beach Master' is gone. You will be fine." Plucked from the water, and safely on the swim grid of the Sea Man, Anika gingerly pulls down her bikini bottom to reveal a severely bruised buttock. The injury looks like a bite from a large dog, every tooth has left a nasty red and purple mark, and a couple of the 'Beach Master's' teeth have punctured her skin.

Mauricio, hearing about the encounter, incredulously comments, "That is unusual. It is only about once a year that someone gets bitten." We are disturbed that Mauricio was not more forthcoming about the dangers of swimming with the 'Beach Master's' harem.

Lonesome George

A trip to the Galapagos Islands would be incomplete without a visit to view the giant saddleback tortoises made famous by Charles Darwin. We begin with a bus trip to the highlands of Santa Cruz. Santa Cruz is one of the few populated islands of the Galapagos archipelago and home to the Charles Darwin Research Station.

A guide leads us along the worn narrow pathways of a private farm in search of the giant dome shaped tortoises. We encounter five of them, a couple of which are half submerged in swampy ponds. One enormous fellow lumbers along bulldozing a path through the scrubby bush.

The next stop on our tour is the Charles Darwin Research Station to meet the infamous 'Lonesome George'. George is thought to be approximately sixty to ninety years old; he weighs eighty-eight kilograms, and is the last of his species.

The tortoises of Pinta Island were decimated by years of over hunting by the fishermen who would stop there. The fisherman would take mostly female turtles because they were easiest to locate when they were laying their eggs on the beaches. The turtles would stay alive in the holds of the boats, without the need for food and water, for up to a year. The population was further decimated by the introduction of domestic goats, which overpopulated the land and ate the vegetation upon which the tortoises relied as a food source.

George is shaped like a Volkswagen beetle and he lumbers awkwardly on stubby flat-footed legs. His neck telescopes phallic-like from a giant carapace, his eyes are beady, and his nose flat, with unprotected nostrils. The research station has been

Posing with the Giant Tortoises of the Galapagos Islands

trying unsuccessfully to mate George with female turtles from Wolf volcano on Isabela Island for over thirty-six years. George has remained stubbornly celibate, prompting the scientists to post a $10,000 reward payable to anyone who can find George a suitable mate.

One of the highlights of our visit to the station is the opportunity to pose for pictures between two of these prehistoric behemoths as they masticate leaves, jaws grinding sideways, beady eyes scanning us curiously.

Captain Freud

When we left Quito, Bob and I knew that we would not be content to do the live-aboard trip and then get back on the plane to mainland Ecuador. Our plan is to spend an extra week and although our movements will be limited, we will relax and do some exploring on our own.

On our arrival back to Pt. Ayora on the main island of Santa Cruz, we go in search of a boat to take us to Isabela Island. Isabela is a large island, with an active volcano, and one of the five inhabited islands in the archipelago.

We find ourselves at the Port Office where we are accosted by a boat captain. He points to a fiberglass boat sitting askew, high and dry on the beach. "That is my boat. Come back at three in the afternoon and I will take you to Isabela." It is a long hot day and we are glad to see three o'clock arrive but unfortunately, the boat is still high and dry. "One hour, come back, we leave in one hour," says our salty weather-beaten captain. What choice did we have? An hour later, still high and dry, six or eight men put their backs to the bow and slide the boat into the water. As we watch, our captain and mate load five twenty-five gallon plastic jerry cans of gasoline onto the deck of the boat.

Two 75 horsepower outboard motors power the twenty-four foot fiberglass shell of a vessel. Open spaghetti wires run the length of the gunnels. Linkage dangles disconnected from the steering wheel at the bow. One engine has a five-foot length of inch and a half plumbing pipe shoved onto the tiller, a white plumbing tee glued to the end of it. The shafts of the engines are joined together with rope to allow the single tiller to steer both engines. Two twenty-five gallon plastic jerry cans, with ill-fitting crude cork stoppers, supply fuel through a narrow black plastic hose. Gasoline bubbles from the over-full jerry cans and onto the deck.

We pile into the boat with three other passengers, all women. 'Captain Freud' sits at the stern. The weatherworn captain has a gravelly cigarette damaged voice and a deeply lined face. He is short and sinewy, reminiscent of Popeye.

Captain Freud pulls the ripcords on the two large outboard motors and we jack rabbit off at full throttle. Fifteen minutes into our journey, we watch in horror as Captain Freud lights a cigarette. Bob is mortified. I nudge him quiet, not wanting to create a scene. Bob breathes a sigh of relief when the butt is extinguished overboard. When Freud lights his second, his head tucked into his shirt to stop the wind, Bob protests. "Es safe, no incendio, no problemo," Freud argues. A short plump grandmotherly passenger sitting across from me rifles through her large handbag extracting a package and she lights a cigarette! Bob is in a state of panic now; his mind is racing, as he plans our escape from the impending explosion and inferno. He tries to calculate whether the present tide and current conditions will drift us to, or away from, the shore. Because of our late departure, darkness threatens to veil our drifting bodies. Sea spray mists over us. The gasoline sloshes side to side in the jerry cans as we bounce, headed for Isabela. Land is not visible on the horizon. Two hours later, we enter the harbour and our captain proudly announces, "Welcome to Vilamila." Bob staggers onto the narrow dock, weak kneed, pale, and vowing, "We won't be travelling back to Santa Cruz with Captain Freud!"

El Nariz Del Diablo – The Nose of the Devil

We are back in Quito. Today is a travel day, a bus ride to Riobamba - simple, right? We taxi to a loop through which busses pull to load and unload passengers. The fifth bus down is nearly full as we board. I beeline for two available seats, near the rear of the bus. The luggage compartment underneath the bus is jam-packed, making it necessary for Bob to tote our bulging backpack on with him and wrestle his way to the back. Two obnoxious young punks, in front of the empty seats, have their seats fully reclined. We have to ask them to rise up enough so we can even get into our seats. The trip is not off to a good start. Within minutes, we are rolling south on the Pan American toll highway.

After travelling for almost three hours, we arrive at the outskirts of a small town called Ambato. Traffic is halted. The swamper on our bus exits to talk to another bus driver. When he returns, our bus u-turns out of the traffic onto a bumpy side road and re-routes us through a small village. We assume that our bus driver knows a bypass. He drives slowly up steep switchback roads taking us from mountain ridge to mountain ridge, and then down into valleys and across bridges where we slowly crawl back up to the ridges again. The bus wends its way, at times feeling like we are going in circles. Passengers on the bus start to get agitated and fidget. Something is not right. As we transit small villages, people on the street corners try to direct the bus in different directions. I spot a sign saying, 'Banos – 15 Kilometers'. We are not supposed to be anywhere near Banos. Travelling up one road, the bus suddenly stops and turns one-eighty! What the hell is going on? The bus is filled beyond capacity and a few poor souls have been standing the entire time. The bus stops at a gas station to refuel, and several passengers disembark to use the restrooms. In extreme pain, I need to pee. "Don't let the bus leave without me," I quip as I exit. Three women are using the restroom. One, who speaks English, explains that there was a taxi strike in Ambato, and they wouldn't let the bus through. We have had to take a detour and our three and a half hour bus trip will now be five hours. As I converse with the women, a small girl squeezes ahead of me in the line-up. *"Rapido!"* I say. My turn, I am near bursting. When I exit the restroom the bus has left the pumps. In a panic I race, heart pounding, to the roadside, boarding the bus on shaky legs. I squirm my way down the aisle. The driver lurches forward, catapulting me full force into one of the standing passengers. Bob tells me the bus tried to leave twice and he had to let out two loud, 'through-the-fingers' whistles before the bus driver reluctantly stopped.

We arrive in Riobamba at two-thirty in the afternoon, two hours later than scheduled.

The inspiration for us to travel to Riobamba is a train called '*El Nariz del Diablo*', 'The Nose of the Devil'. The train is a tourist attraction and is touted as 'the most difficult railway in the world to build'. Construction started in Guayaquil, on the coast, in 1899 and was temporarily halted when it encountered a near perpendicular wall called '*El Nariz del Diablo*'. In an amazing feat of railway engineering, a zigzag was carved out of the rock to allow the train to advance and reverse itself to a height great enough that it could continue to Alausi. The train reached Alausi in September 1902 and finally, Riobamba in July 1905.

The morning is cold and drizzly and the draw of this particular trip is that the tourists are encouraged to ride on the roof of the train. We climb a cold steel ladder up the side of the red tin roofed boxcar, our rented cushions dangling from our wrists. Settling in on the frigid corrugated roof, I secretly wonder just what I was thinking when I imagined this would be fun. As I said previously, the rail reached Riobamba in 1905 and seemingly, no repairs or maintenance have been done on the tracks since. The first couple of hours are uneventful. We *click-clack* through terraced green farmland, children rush to wave waiting eagerly for the tourists to toss suckers and candies. Vendors balance precariously on a narrow wooden center walkway, back and forth, back and forth, *"Lollies for the kids? Lollies, for the keeds? Cinco for one dollar."* We stop briefly for a bathroom break, at Alausi; our trip from here will take us through *'El Nariz del Diablo'*. Not far from Alausi, the train lurches coming to an abrupt halt, and the engine drops at a twisted angle from the boxcar behind it. Several trainmen bail out, jamming rocks in a gap in the rail, allowing each boxcar to bump its' way over. "Do you see what they are doing?" Bob says on the edge of hysteria. Farther down the track, once again, the train grinds to a halt and the trainmen jump off to throw chunky boulders off the track. Now, the ride is starting to become exciting. We travel along a narrow ridge overlooking a deep gorge to the river far below. The train starts an elaborate zigzag through the Nose

Tourists Riding on the Roof of the Train
– El Nariz del Diablo

of the Devil, forward and backward, forward and backward, forward and backward, as we start our descent into the canyon. A sudden stop and the trainmen bail once again with their shovels; a small slide is blocking the tracks halting our zigzag pattern. At the canyon floor, we all disembark for photos before starting our slow ascent back up 'The Devil's Nose', to Alausi.

Bob is incensed by the disrepair of the tracks. Spikes are missing, ties are splintered and splayed by the weight of the top-heavy train, and he feels it is just a short matter of time before a trainload of tourists perishes, tumbling into the steep rocky canyon.

It was an exhilarating day. In a conversation with some tourists two weeks later, they told us that the train was stopped from running for safety reasons, just a week following our ride through 'The Nose of the Devil'. I really hate to admit it but I guess sometimes Bob is right.

Banos - In the Shadow of Fiery Tungurahua

Banos is a small town of 30,000 people. It sits in a valley over-shadowed by a belching fiery adversary, the active Tungurahua volcano. In October of 1999, the town was forced to evacuate under order of the Ecuadorian government. Scientists issued an orange alert declaring the volcano could erupt at any time. Three months later, without the blessing of the government, the townspeople slowly started to filter back. Banos, with its sulfur smelling hot springs, remains a popular tourist destination in Ecuador, despite the continuing threat from Tungurahua.

The inn at which we are staying in Banos is called the Villa Gertrudis. It is an enormous old wooden mansion. When we arrive, we walk up a few concrete steps and ring the doorbell. The door is thick solid wood with heavy black iron hinges and a tiny peephole. The ringing summons our hostess; the door creaks open. A stooped grey haired woman, wearing a white apron and house slippers, ushers us into the foyer, bolting the massive door behind us. She leads us through the hallway to an enormous room with ten-foot high ceilings and thick-planked floors, buffed to an ebony sheen. The high king-size bed has crisp, white cotton sheets. A top sheet is turned down over a golden satin comforter. The room is lovely but the atmosphere, creepy. It is reminiscent of a scene from the Steven King movie 'The Shining'. I expect Jack Nicholson to axe his way through our dark wooden door at any moment. A silver skeleton key sits in the keyhole.

In the morning when we arrive in the dining room for breakfast, two places are set on a linen tablecloth; we are the only guests in the bed and breakfast. The dining room is massive. A woman wearing what resembles a yellow and white nurses' uniform emerges through a swinging door carrying two plates. There are no windows into the kitchen. Bob and I glance sideways at each other, how did she know we had arrived? We eat nervously, the Lord and Lady of this eerie manor.

Each time we exit or enter our strange accommodations, we have to ring the doorbell. Are we guests or prisoners? Only our white haired warden knows for sure.

In the afternoon, we stop at a *Pasteleria* for cake and coffee. Outside on the sidewalk a thin, wizened old man, wearing rumpled clothes, leads a goat with a piece of twine. A small dark haired girl accompanies him. He stops on the street corner and binds together the rear legs of the goat. Roughly, he flicks the teats of the nanny and he squeezes milk into a tall soiled glass. Using this one glass, he sells warm servings of goat milk to eager customers who down the opaque body temperature fluid on the spot then pass the glass back to the old man, to be refilled for the next customer.

We meet an American family on a street corner in town. They are trying to negotiate a deal on quad motorcycles for the afternoon. "Would you like to join us?" the father asks. "Sure, why not, sounds like fun!" Half an hour later, the six of us are cruising down the highway. The machines are fully automatic and easy to ride, but it is a little unnerving when trucks and buses approach from behind and pass us. We are having a blast and after a long ride, we come to the first of several tunnels. After doing a light check, we realize almost all of our headlights are working but few of us have working taillights. The tunnel is short and we can see light at the other end, so, off we go. It is inky dark but we pass through without incident.

The second tunnel is an entirely different story. As we enter it is dark, and there is no light visible from the opposite end. The ceiling is craggy limestone; water rains down on us from above. Cars, trucks, and buses pass precariously close from both directions. With a sigh of relief, we burst forth into the sunlight, and continue our journey, our courage bolstered by our survival.

The trip is magnificent. Gorgeous waterfalls spew out of the mountainside cascading into the river below. A stifling twenty-minute hike takes us to our last stop, *'Cascada Pailon del Diablo'* (The Devil's Cauldron). The falls thunder down a steep verdant crack in the face of the granite cliff, split in two, and re-unite in a frothy pool. Basking in the over spraying

Riding Quads in Banos.

mist, we close our eyes, cooled by the refreshing shower. Our reverie is cut short by impending darkness and we rush, panting, back to the quads.

In the parking lot, a man approaches me speaking Spanish, and all I can understand is that he is saying something about the lights on the bikes. He is with a young woman who speaks English and she explains that they were behind us in one of the tunnels and the driver had to slam on his brakes to avoid hitting us. Only one taillight was visible. I thank her and ask her, "Can we bypass the tunnels?" She replies, "Yes," and then as an afterthought, she says, "God bless you." I counter, "Thank-you, we may need your blessings today!" Back on the quads, we race as fast as we can in an attempt to beat nightfall, bypassing the first small tunnel. At the long tunnel, we bypass to the left, along a narrow gravel road, taking us through a small village perched at the edge of the canyon. Dark haired children run to greet us shouting, *"Hola,"* as they wave. Runoff water rains down on our helmeted heads as we pass under craggy overhangs. Regrouping on the edge of the highway, Bob and I switch jackets. He will take up the rear, wearing my white jacket, hopefully making the group more visible in the waning light. When we reach the final tunnel, we discover there is no bypass. One of the young American boys enters the tunnel and I follow close wearing the black jacket. The taillight on my quad is not functioning. I silently pray the light, quickly approaching behind me, is one of the other bikes. As I exit the tunnel, a taxi races past blaring its horn!

The next day, we sit in the yellow sulfur-smelling pool of the hot springs warming our stiff muscles and discussing our risk taking and poor judgment. Why is it that we behave like unruly children when we are travelling? But really, what would life be without risk?

Tungurahua behaves itself while we are in Banos, only occasionally burping and spewing ashy clouds and molten fireballs into the night sky.

CHAPTER 10

Kenya – Africa

Freaking Afreaka

February of 2006, we venture to Africa for the first time. We book with GAP Adventures for safety reasons, uncertain as to the difficulty of travelling through Africa unescorted. The following is an account of our first delectable taste of the Dark Continent.

It is one p.m. and we have just boarded a KLM flight to Amsterdam where we will catch a connecting flight to Nairobi, Kenya. Anticipating this adventure has consumed every waking, sleeping, daydreaming moment. Bob is dozing in the seat beside me. I shall miss the children and hope that our new baby grandson, Kaiden, will not change too much in the seven weeks we are gone. The plane taxis down the runway and lifts off into a clear blue sky.

We are seated in row forty, second row from the rear of the plane. Behind us sit two Middle Eastern men; two more sit two rows in front of us and to their left, across the aisle, two more. I am comforted by the fact they stuff two large red Danier Leather shopping bags into the overhead bin. You wouldn't shop at Danier Leather if you were on a suicide mission - would you? For lunch, we are served the usual airline fare and after trays are cleared away, we sit sated and sleepy in our seats. The Middle Eastern man behind me starts a singsong prayer to Allah. He drones on for fifteen minutes rocking back and forth, as he chants. I envision him leaping up at any moment and declaring, "I have a bomb!" I sit listening to their mucous filled guttural conversation and I swear to 'Allah' the only words I understand are Jihad, Hamas, and Aljazeera. I am thrilled to report that many hours later, we land safely in Amsterdam, and our only disturbance was their persistent kicking at the backs of our seats.

We are in Schipol Airport with a two-hour layover before our flight to Nairobi. Why are airports so discombobulating? You always feel confused, tired, and heady, but at least English is spoken here and we have found our gate, with time to spare. Our pockets are stuffed with 11,000 Kenyan shillings. Our anticipation mounts.

The flight to Nairobi is uneventful save a fair bit of turbulence as we cross the African continent. I sit beside a nineteen-year-old American boy who reminds me of my friend Joy's son, Andrew. He is a giant, six feet plus, and sits folded and uncomplaining in the seat next to me. He is with a group of twelve led by an American neurosurgeon. In the group are several nurses and they are off to do Missionary work in a clinic founded and funded by the neurosurgeon. The clinic sits approximately thirty miles from the city of Nairobi. The young man's eyes sparkle with excited anticipation and I wonder whether he has any inkling as to the toll on his psyche that working with broken humanity will take. I silently wish him well.

Nairobi airport is a pleasant surprise. It is large and modern, the glass and steel of any big city airport. Our new backpacks arrive safely and after loading up like pack mules, we pass through the double glass doors to a waiting throng of bus and taxi drivers. Our driver from *eastafricashuttles.com* waves a sign, *'Bob & Rosalie'*, catching our attention almost immediately. We lock eyes with George; his cream coloured Tilley-style hat frames his round, midnight black face. It feels as if an old friend has met us and mentally I pat myself on the back for prearranging our pick up. George hurries us out of the airport to his taxi. The night is a warm 21 degrees Celsius with a soft wind blowing. George drives us expertly through the sparse night traffic, asking us questions about Canada and we about Kenya. We pass a fender-bender and notice the people milling around the scene. A cop in fatigues directs traffic, a rifle casually slung over his shoulder.

Our hotel is what we expect; not somewhere that we would remotely consider staying at in Vancouver. The area is very downtown eastside. Taxis choke the perimeter, too many to serve too few tourists. The drivers lean against the cars, their dark faces shadowy in the neon sign of the hotel. Bob pays George in the car avoiding the woman begging just outside the taxi door, in the poorly lit street.

The lobby of the Kenya Comfort Inn is small, crowded, and filled with other tourists trying to check-in. We meet Laura, a young single woman from Ottawa who is part of our tour group. Keys in hand, we ascend in the rickety caged elevator to the fourth floor. A crude iron bar gate that is covered many times over with thick coats of paint, secures each floor. Bob unlocks the gate to our floor and our escort takes us down a worn narrow hallway to room 409, the shoebox which will be our home for the next two nights. The room is just one step up from a hostel with a private, cramped bathroom and a surprisingly comfortable queen bed. We settle in and head back down to the first floor restaurant for a snack and our first local beer.

The restaurant is open and welcoming. A chef cooks at an open hooded grill. Steam and aromatic smells fill the room. Service is slow, African time.

Back in our room, we chat trying to unwind from our hectic day. We fall into bed for a fitful sleep to the drone of raucous drinking and partying. We are startled awake by a vicious argument in the alley between a prostitute and her pimp. Random gunshots pierce the quiet of the night.

Nairobi looks less frightening in the daylight. We shower and head to the first floor for breakfast. After breakfast we wander to a local market a couple of blocks away. Shopping is not on our agenda, we just want to browse and check out the wares. Starting out relaxed, we explain to the shopkeepers, "We are not ready to shop yet, we have just arrived." In the beginning, they are respectful but a little insistent. They are curious about where we are from and proud to offer us information about Kenya. The farther we get into the market the more persistent they become. Exiting into a small alley, we wander through the butcheries, the shops selling chickens, goat, fish followed by the vegetable and fruit vendors. We circle back into an alley of souvenir vendors trying to find our way back into the main market. The situation is getting uncomfortable. We find it difficult to get past a shop; the men jostle for our attention in a deliberate attempt to separate Bob and me. Overwhelmed, and a little scared, Bob and I now separated, beeline for the exit. Breathing a sigh of relief, we find ourselves reunited on the street.

We meet with our GAP group in the evening, all Canadians; Bob, and I from British Columbia and the rest of the group from the Toronto area. The majority of the group is the age of our children. The trip, 'Cultural Kenya', is a new trip for GAP Adventures. It is an inaugural run, and therefore, we will be well looked after. GAP has sent Stephan, the head of their European office in Spain, to accompany us. Our African guide is Ken, who arrives late for our meeting. An African, on African time. A driver and a cook will also accompany us.

After the meeting, Ken escorts us to a restaurant for some local fare. The place is lively and loud and there are no white faces evident in the establishment. We dine outside at a large table in a cooling, evening breeze. The dinner choices are beef, chicken, or fish with rice except that they are out of chicken. Bob takes one look at the whole crispy fried fish, vacant eyeballs staring back, and he decides, he can forgo food. I have the fish in a yummy coconut sauce; Bob has a small plate of steamed rice. He will be the one arriving home thinner.

You Can't Bicycle in a Buffalo Herd

"Dear Diarrhea"… my god how to I begin to do today justice? The Christmas my granddaughter was five I gave her a flowery, vinyl-covered diary with a tiny silver lock, and key. Marenda hugged it to her chest and rocking back and forth said, "Thankyou for the diarrhea Nana." Diary has been diarrhea, ever since.

Our prompt eight a.m. departure leaves at nine-thirty a.m.; we are all, now on Africa time. The luggage is loaded onto the roof of a small bus and covered with a large canvas tarp. Buzzing with excitement, we all pile onto the bus and we are off. About three blocks down the road, we stop at the Nairobi City Market to change our American dollars into Kenyan shillings. The entire transaction has a shady feel to it. Two men come from the market to the door of the bus; one of them pulls a large wad of bills from the pocket of his baggy pants. They trade us sixty-nine Kenyan shillings for one American dollar, not an excellent rate, but a fair one. As the bus pulls away from the market, our African guide Ken says, "If there is a problem, there is no problem." We assume this strange statement to mean, if any of us has received counterfeit notes, he will take care of them for us.

We drive about an hour to a rest stop affording us a fantastic view of the Great Rift Valley. We dodge hawkers to take photos of the spectacular view. An hour and a half later, we arrive at the hotel where we will spend the next two nights in a small town called Naivasha. The Naivasha Silver Hotel has a stucco façade painted in cotton candy pink and teal green. Even the rocks edging the parking lot are painted, striped, in both colours. The quaint little village is bustling; a waterman sits on the side of the road, his three donkeys hooked to a crude cart. He sucks on a thick siphon hose to fill jugs from the large barrels on the cart. Another waterman rides down a steep incline in front of a large wooden wheelbarrow affair. He is the donkey, and he uses his feet as brakes. The weight of the water periodically lifts him, comically, right off the road. The town is less edgy than Nairobi and the people go about their business not at all interested in us. We are just a curiosity here and it is refreshing.

After settling into our rooms, it is decided that we will spend the afternoon biking into a place called Hells Gate. Piling into the bus, we drive to a place called 'Fisherman's Camp' to rent bikes. The journey is interesting. Much of the highway is under construction, and the dust is so fine that it often completely obscures visibility. A large Tusker Beer truck lies on its side like a dead animal. It sits, abandoned, with no sign of emergency crews or vehicles. We run an obstacle course; a maze of rocks placed to slow traffic, the bus driver often unsure of which way to turn.

Arriving at the camp, we are fitted with our rattletrap bikes. "This one has no brakes. This one has two flat tires. This one the seat is too high," I whine as Bob turns himself inside out trying to placate me. At three-thirty p.m., after choosing the best of the worst, we leave the camp and head out in the hottest part of the day. Insane! The climb up to the main road is hot and dusty. We pedal the bikes through a small village. In Kenya, at any time of the day, people are everywhere. Some folks sit solitary and idle, some chat, catching up on local gossip, and there is always a steady stream of people going somewhere. Women wrapped in multi-hued sarongs and headscarves carry jugs and baskets perched on their heads, their backs ramrod straight. Men, wearing ill fitting dusty tattered suits and riding old tubular bicycles, focus on their destination. Others walk a slow but determined pace, going where? Children frolic as only children can, playing with sticks or balls fashioned from twined together plastic bags. All the children holler out incessantly, *"Haow are you? Haow are you? Haow are you?"* waving to us as we pass.

The road to the park gate is dusty and steep. At the gate, we pay our fifteen American dollars, to enter Hells Gate National Park, and we begin our journey *'to hell and back'*.

The only hazard on the flat dusty road is the soft powdery ruts that temporarily cause me to lose control of my steering. We ride through dry grassland dotted with herds of animals. The scene is surreal; zebras, gazelles, oryx, warthogs, and baboons flank our rutted path. Unfazed, they raise their heads, eyeing us curiously as we pass. Dust as fine as baby powder puffs around our wheels. Taking a short rest at the entrance to the gorge, we abandon our bicycles, and hike a steep trail down, down, down into the gorge. The steps are steep and slippery and at times, we have to straddle or cross over the small stream. Passing trickling thermally heated waterfalls; we stick our hands into near boiling puddles eroded into the sandstone riverbed. Outcroppings with warm and cold showers rain down on our hot, sweaty, dust covered bodies. We work our way up to a spectacular viewpoint and eventually circle back to our bikes. I am exhausted, spent, finished. I cannot imagine how I can possibly get back on my bike and pedal the eleven kilometers back to camp. Dusk is looming.

Just before we mount our bicycles for the return journey, we talk to a park guide. Earlier that day, he was escorting two tourists on a game walk, when from out of the trees, a buffalo charged. He managed to swing his machete, hitting it

Cape Buffalo

on the snout, but not before the buffalo gored him in the thigh.

The guide shows us the hole in his khaki pants, and the round crimson wound the horn inflicted!

Back on the bikes, "I am exhausted, I am not sure I can do this," I declare to Bob. Before he can respond I say, "I know, I know. There is no choice." Off we go. The buffalo, which were hiding in the shade of the trees in the heat of the day, are now out grazing the grasslands in the evening cool. "Stick together," caution our guides. I cannot keep up. Gradually we fall behind, Bob, me, and the rear guide. "Go quickly!" the guide commands. I am pedaling with all I have. I hit a soft dusty rut and fall off my bike. "Keep pedaling!" the guide demands. Struggling to my feet, I cry, "Bob, I don't think I can do this!" But I must. Heart pounding, I use all of my reserve strength, and the three of us pass safely. This is not our only close encounter, three more times the group stops to wait for us to catch up; there are more buffalos to pass. Each time we fall behind, my heart thunders in my chest.

Before we left on our ride, I was talking to one of the girls named Allison. She told me a fractured fable that went like this, " When being chased by a predator, zebras will only run as fast as the slowest in the herd. They all stay together for protection. You know, safety in numbers." Where was the rest of our GAP group when I was faltering on my bike? Our group was certainly *NOT ZEBRAS!*

We did get out and we did beat the darkness, but barely. We bounced home dodging rocks and vehicles and after a shower and dinner, I fell into bed exhausted.

On the bike ride home through the village, the children, once again, lined the streets shouting, *"Haow are you?" "Haow are you?" "Haow are you?"* Feeling exhilarated and spent at the same time, their little singsong voices brought me to tears.

CHAPTER 11

Uganda - Africa

King Kong

Our flight from Nairobi, Kenya to Entebbe, Uganda was due to leave at six-ten p.m. We board about thirty minutes late and now, a further thirty minutes later, we are still sitting on the tarmac while they try to repair 'a minor technical problem'. The captain announces that we will have to disembark; the problem is more serious than expected. "A new plane will be available at nine p.m., sorry for the inconvenience. Snacks will be served at the gate." Back in the holding lounge, moments later, a new announcement, "Ladies and gentlemen, sorry for the delay, we will now re-board the plane." "The same plane! Wait a minute, is this thing safe!" I screech at Bob.

Fifty-five minutes later, we land safely in Entebbe. A ten-dollar taxi ride takes us to Sofie's Hotel. The room is clean and large with a television but no running water. Power is turned off for the night. The dam on Lake Victoria cannot supply enough power for the town. A large yellow jerry can of water sits beside a white washbasin in the shower. Welcome to Uganda.

In the morning, we meet with a tour company representative Jane, and our guide, Steffi. We have booked the trip through GAP Adventures but they have contracted it out to a local company. Jane tells us that the itinerary, set out by GAP in their brochure, will not be followed. Two gay men from Chicago will join us, Ernie and Clintess (no, I didn't make that up). They are pleasant enough but Ernie is slightly obsessive and he is upset that our itinerary has been changed. Will his office be able to reach him if necessary? Jane, the company rep, informs him curtly that he has to expect "glitches" in Uganda. Jane tells us, "There is an election here on February 23rd and you may be witness to some political unrest. In the last election, the phone lines were shut down." In the days to come, it becomes evident that this is a candy-coated version of the possible dangers that lurk.

Our transport for the tour is a rugged Toyota Land Cruiser and with just Steffi and the four of us, it will be comfortable.

Uganda surprises us in contrast to Kenya. It is green and lush; the countryside is cleaner and less populated, the people are more prosperous, and their homes are pleasant and better built.

The road is hard packed rusty-coloured earth, washboard, and full of potholes with deep ruts worn by rivers of muddy water that flow during the rainy season. We cross a so-called 'floating bridge'. The crossing is edged with three-foot high red concrete cylinders delineated with foot markers to help the vehicles navigate during the monsoons. The bridge does not float; the cars float! We travel along mountain ridges peering into sunlit valleys. The steep valley walls are terraced and planted with crops of bananas, tea, cabbage, cassava, rice, potatoes, and tomatoes. Each crop, a unique shade of green, blankets the land creating a dramatic growing patchwork quilt.

Five days later, we arrive at our destination, Bwindi Impenetrable Forest. Sounds ominous, doesn't it? As soon as we unload our packs, the sky opens up. It starts with rolling thunder followed by flashes of lightning and then a deluge of biblical proportions. The wind blows the rain sideways, driving us from the covered shelter deeper into the protection of the building. The rain turns from giant droplets into marble-size hail. We are held prisoner by the storm for half an hour as the roadway is turned into a raging torrent. Suddenly, the hail stops and the skies brighten; a mist lifts off the dense mountainside jungle and the storm is over.

Our tiny cabin is perched on the hillside overlooking the forest. The shuttered windows picture frame a verdant vista. We have truly travelled to the edge of the world.

Dinner is served at seven-thirty p.m. on a table covered in white linen. Saucy chicken follows tomato soup with warm rolls, topped off with a dessert of fried bananas, and washed down by a bottle of chilled South African wine. When we retire to our cabin, a kerosene lantern, placed on our porch, lights the pathway. Staff have turned down our beds and inserted full hot water bottles between the cold sheets. Decadent!

Getting ourselves to this place and time was expensive; the park permit fee alone cost us five hundred American dollars each. Will it be worth it?

Early morning, Steffi drives us to the park entrance to meet our guide. Twenty-four tourists are divided into three groups of eight. Our group will visit 'H Group', the Habinhanja Group consisting of twenty-two gorillas, the only group with two silverback males. Trackers are out early locating the gorilla groups and are in constant radio contact with the guides. We are told that the hike into the forest could be up to four hours and we are only allowed a one-hour visit on our five hundred dollar permit. We are driven twenty-two kilometers up the mountain to begin our hike.

An endangered species, there are only six hundred to six hundred and forty mountain gorillas left in the world. These are the ones brought to the attention of the world by Dian Fossey. She lived with, and studied the gorillas over several decades beginning in the 1960's. In 1983, she published the manuscript, Gorillas in the Mist, documenting her life with them. On

December 27, 1985, she was found murdered in her cabin in the Virunga Mountains of Rwanda. Hit twice on the head and slashed with a machete, the circumstance of her murder has never been fully resolved. She was buried beside her favorite gorilla, Digit who died in 1977.

Military guards armed with high-powered rifles accompany us. In February of 1999, eight tourists were kidnapped and brutally murdered by Hutu rebels in Uganda's, Bwindi Impenetrable Forest National Park. Two Americans, four Brits, and two New Zealanders were hacked to death with machetes and axes. News of these grisly murders spread quickly around the world. The Hutus were from neighboring Rwanda and part of the ethnic extremists responsible for the 1994 genocide where over 500,000 Tutsis were massacred.

Two bushwhacking guides also accompany us. The trail is spongy and slick, low-lying vines entangle our ankles. We ford a wide stream following close behind the trackers. Twenty minutes later, we are within three hundred meters of the gorillas. In hushed whispers, the guides run through the rules; no talking, no eating or drinking, no flash photography, no making eye contact with the silverback male. The jungle is dense and it is raining. I spot my first gorilla, dangerously close in the thickets. My heart stops. The massive animal sits on its haunches directly in front of me. Suddenly, gorillas are all around us. Branches crash and break as they make their way to the forest floor. The smaller of the two silverbacks wrestles with a female in an attempt to mate. Two juvenile males swing around the base of a tree trunk, chest beating, emanating a *pop, pop, pop.* A plump female rolls on her back, her baby plays at her side. A youth bounces on a springy sapling, playing in the bush like a human child. An adult sits near a tree picking his nose and eating what he finds. The rain continues to fall and my camera complains about the lack of light, I cannot get a good picture. I abandon my camera awed, and resigned to the fact that we are not meant to capture some of life's moments.

He materializes in the mist. King Kong. The dominant silverback, two hundred and fifty kilograms of brawn, sits on his haunches. He surveys the forest; he knows we are there, watching. We bow our heads in respect and fear, as we peer through the branches. His head is dark and elongated with black eyes inset over a flattened nose; a swath of silver covers his wide back, ruby red lips circle a rose coloured mouth. Black finger-nailed, hairy, digits fondle a leaf before he stuffs it into his mouth. A female rolls provocatively at his side in the trampled grass.

We are so privileged.

Election Day

A guide takes us on a morning walk. A military park guard leads in the front and one flanks our rear. Both have army issued semi-automatic rifles, in questionable shape, slung over their shoulders. Our guide walks us to Buhoma Village at the edge of the forest, to visit a traditional healer. From the Congo, he wears a wide brimmed hat made from animal hide and an animal hide apron, and when he sees my Canada hat, he attempts speaking French to me. I am embarrassed that I cannot communicate with him. An important member of the commu- nity, he grows healing herbs that he mixes into concoctions to cure a mixed bag of maladies; everything from snakes bites to pneumonia, exorcising evil spirits to curing male impotency. He works in conjunc- tion with the local hos- pital; both refer patients to each other, a fright- ening thought.

Traditional Healer – Bwindi Impenetrable Forest

Next stop on our tour is the brewery where bananas are brewed into wine, beer, and a clear fluid that tastes like gin. Green bananas are buried in an open pit to start the fermentation process. They are then dug up and put into a long dugout trough with shredded banana leaves where the brew-master, barefoot, stomps the bananas into a mushy pulp. Roasted sorghum is added to the mix to complete the fermentation process. We decline a taste of the nasty brew.

The final stop is at a pygmy village. The pygmies were displaced from the forest by the government when Bwindi was declared a national park. Shy and elusive, before the government displaced them, they hunted for food in the forest wearing only animal skins. Numbering only thirty-eight, the government gave them sixteen acres of land, constructed homes, a hospital, and a school for them. The pygmies perform traditional songs and dances for our tourist dollars. I am saddened to see these proud people reduced to a tourist attraction.

After lunch, we pack into the land cruiser. Our tour is ending. Today is Election Day. Every few miles we see long line-ups of locals at the polling stations. People we pass show their political

Displaced Pygmies – Bwindi
Impenetrable Forest

affiliation, a thumb in the air for the incumbent president, a 'V' for the opposition. Steffi, sitting on the fence, wisely displays both. People are everywhere and the tension is evident. Arriving in Kabale, Steffi drives us to the Whitehorse Inn, isolated high on a hill overlooking the town. Our room has a television and we tune it to the BBC. On the news, we discover that it is the first parliamentary and presidential election in twenty-six years. The incumbent president, Museveni, had changed the rules allowing him to remain in power. The opposition, Besigye, was in exile for four years and when he returned to Uganda, he was arrested for alleged treason, theft, and rape. We now understand the tensions. Before dinner, we walk across the manicured lawns to the edge of the property. Yelling, horn honking, and revelry filters up the hillside as each ballot is held in the air and counted. Back in the lobby, three armed military, rifles resting casually between their legs, listen to walkie-talkies. They are there to guard a contingent of World Vision workers hiding out in the hotel. Rain starts to pelt down on the metal roof and a fierce thunder and lightening storm erupts. I hope the rain will dampen the revelry in town keeping them safely away from our sanctuary.

The next morning, as we depart, there is a guarded peace in the streets. People clutch cheap transistor radios awaiting election results. We stop at 10:30 for a break and Steffi disappears. He tells us on his return that he has been checking with his office as to whether it is safe to travel through Kampala. "It will be fine," he states. However, he then relates a story about vehicles being rocked and a truck set on fire. Steffi bypasses downtown Kampala as a precaution. We arrive in Entebbe at five p.m. unscathed. The full election results will not be in until tomorrow, the day we fly out.

CHAPTER 12

Zanzibar – Tanzania, Africa

Zunny, Zandy, Zanzibar

Zanzibar is the perfect finale to our African adventure, ten days of rest and relaxation. Every day is much the same as the previous one and we fall into a comfortable routine. Each morning I stake out my chair early, under the thatched shade umbrella. I can no longer bear the sun, the doxycycline I am taking for malaria has made me extremely sun sensitive, and my legs and forearms are covered in red blisters. Bob, wearing cotton pajama pants, scours the water's edge for shells. I read and occasionally scan the beach, watching for his familiar gait. Sometimes his shell bag is empty. Sometimes it bulges and I wait excitedly to see what treasures he has found. We sit and talk for a while and then stroll next door for lunch where we have become expected. They affectionately call Bob, Baboo, which means grandfather.

In the afternoon, we stroll the beach together waiting for the tide to reverse and fill the pool that has emptied with the receding tide. We swim in the late afternoon in lapping waves that are warmed by sugar sand that has baked in the relentless African sun. We dry in the warm breeze and then shower off the sand and salt.

Where shall we have dinner? The choices are few. Zanzibar is not ready for tourists. The red wine is cold, the white wine is gone, we have no avocado, no eggs today, no beer served here…we are Muslim. At night, the Masai sit at the bar next door, smoking dope. During the day, they patrol the beaches riding mountain bikes, dressed in full regalia, chatting with each other on cell phones, from Bwejuu through Paje to Jambiani. In Bweju, where there is a resort that caters to Italian tourists, the Masai speak Italian. *"Ciao, ciao, ciao"*, they call out to the tourists.

In the morning, the seaweed ladies follow the tide out. They sit in roped off patches stuffing wet weed into white sacs. As the afternoon tide fills the lagoon, they drag the heavy sacs to the water's edge, hoisting them onto their heads. Their crooked bodies plod through the wet sand, up the beach, to dry the seaweed in the sun. It is sold for pennies a kilo and exported to Japan. Fishermen launch dugout *dhows*, and wearing a mask and snorkel they prod the reef with a sharpened stick bringing in octopus for the lunch and dinner menus. Young boys drag a net through the shallows as their buddies yell and smack the water with sticks to drive schools of shiners into the net. They drag the net up onto the beach and scramble to gather up the tiny flipping silver fish. Women, draped in cotton kangas, saunter by, *"Jambo,* massage?"

Everyday, like clockwork, the lagoon drains. Everyday, like clockwork, the lagoon fills. A giant orange moon rises on the horizon as a light wind blows and the sky fills with sparkling diamonds.

Saturday afternoon, a young boy approaches us on the beach selling shells. "I won't buy your shells but I have a gift for you," I tell him. I give him several small trinkets, a Canada pin, a matchbox car, and two flashing pins. His English is poor, *"Take to Canada. One, two, three, Canada tomorrow. Okay? Canada good. Zanzibar, no good. No Toys. One, two, three, Canada tomorrow. Okay?"* His requests escalate. He wants Bob's pants, his hat, his money, and more toys. "No, sorry. You stay in school, work hard, and get a job," I admonish. Bob bends in the surf to pick something up. It looks like a triangular shaped amber rock. He passes it to me. It is light and I bounce it in my hand and squeeze it, showing it to my new eleven-year-old friend. He seems perplexed by it. The rock breaks in half and it is clear like hardened tree sap. *"I know. Hotel. Fire. Plate. Burn,"* our shadow exclaims. He motions with his hands, breathes in, saying, *"Ahhh."* He repeats, *"Fire. Plate."* Big sniff, *"Ahhh."* "It must be eucalyptus sap," I say to Bob. *"Can I have?"* asks my new friend. He slips the two pieces into the pocket of his tattered shorts.

It is not until we are back at the hotel that the light bulb comes on. The 'rock' was a narcotic of some description.

Two things terrify me. First, I almost threw the strange rock into my bag of shells to pack innocently into my luggage and second, I gave, what was probably a lump of opium, to an eleven-year-old boy on the beach!

CHAPTER 13

Myanmar (Burma) – Southeast Asia

Men in Skirts

March of 2007, we travel back in time to a place so ensconced in the past that it is difficult to believe we are still in the twenty first century.

We begin our journey in the capital city of Yangon, once again with a GAP group. Great Adventure People's inaugural trip into Myanmar, it is a controversial move. An iron-fisted military junta rules Myanmar and the jury is out as to whether tourism is helping the people of one of the poorest countries in the world or whether it is condoning a corrupt government. The government restricts tourist movements and it is the first place we have been where it is impossible to get Internet access. I pre-warned the children that we might be incommunicado for ten days.

The government also controls the currency. The 'official government exchange rate' is six Kyats for one American dollar. Our hotel desk offers *twelve hundred* Kyats for one American dollar. Our taxi driver tells us the moneychangers at the market will give us twelve hundred and forty to twelve hundred and eighty Kyats for one American dollar! Black market money abounds.

We are staying in a hotel called the Panorama, in Yangon. Soon after we are checked in, our GAP guide, Tristan, knocks on our door. Tristan is of Chinese descent, however he speaks no Chinese, was raised in New Zealand, and has a thick kiwi accent. Tristan will find it more difficult to blend in here than we do, as obvious occidental tourists. Tristan has arrived a week before to familiarize himself with the city and the culture. He gives us directions to the market and assures us that it is safe to trade our dollars into Kyats there.

We head towards the market, walking the city on sidewalks dotted with beggars, many of who are maimed. After many years of travel to third world countries, the souls of numerous beggars scar my psyche but none more than a woman I pass on a sidewalk in Yangon. She sits cross-legged, her soiled clothing hanging on an emaciated skeletal frame, her bra-less breasts flattened and devoid of mother's milk. Her eyes are dead and she thrusts her cupped hand hopefully skyward. An infant swaddled in a filthy blanket lies loosely in her lap; its eyes glazed and opaque in sunken sockets. Skin taut over an orange-size shrunken head, the tiny baby is stiff and devoid of life, dead or near death. No amount of money or medical intervention could save it. I close my downcast eyes and swallow a sob.

On our way to the market, we pass a theatre with billboards advertising old Chuck Norris and Sylvester Stallone movies. The market is housed in a large two-story warehouse filled with 'Government Licensed' jewelry stores and clothing shops. We are soon accosted, "Do you want to exchange money? Sir, money exchange?"

Tristan has told us we should get around 1260 Kyats for one American dollar. We rebuff several moneychangers offering less and finally agree on 1250 Kyats per dollar. Our skirt clad conspirator spirits us off to an area of relative privacy, plopping a worn black leather valise with brass latches onto the counter. All of the men in Myanmar wear longhis, which are yards of material expertly knotted at the waist. The material hangs to the ankles swishing back and forth and provides absolute and unencumbered comfort. The tall, lean, elderly man opens the valise revealing bricks of banded money. Two hundred American dollars buys us 250,000 Kyats and the largest denomination is 1000. Overwhelmed by the large bricks of bills, I hand Bob a stack and we begin counting. I get flustered and loose count, forcing me to restart. "Hurry up," our cohort in crime demands. "I will not cheat you. I am missing out on business!" Frustrated he declares, "I will check your bills!" And he does, scraping his long, chipped yellowed fingernail across them and checking for imperfections in an attempt to allay our suspicion. Satisfied, we part company stuffing the huge wads of stiff bills into my purse and into Bob's pockets.

The Golden Rock Pagoda

There are only eight of us in our GAP group. One American from San Francisco, Roger, one Canadian expat from London, Simon, a couple from British Columbia, Peter and Lynda, one Dane, Hendrick, whom we affectionately nickname Danish, Bob and I, and our guide, Tristan.

In the morning, a local tour company picks us up in a new air-conditioned minibus for a long five-hour journey to Kyaiktiyo and the mystical Golden Rock Pagoda. All Buddhists in Myanmar aspire to completing a pilgrimage to the Golden Rock Pagoda, it equates to their Mecca.

We motor through bucolic farmland and small villages. Along the roadside, we pass an all women railway crew hauling buckets of jagged rocks and lying ties and rails in the hot afternoon sun.

A road crew toils over forty-five gallon drums of tar bubbling over an open fire. Tin dippers on bamboo poles are used to spread the noxious brew over hand scattered pea gravel. Wooden horse drawn wagons, filled with golden hay, bump down dusty side roads.

When we arrive at the base of the mountain, people are everywhere. Trucks are arriving and leaving as they shuttle the pilgrims and tourists part way up the steep mountain. We climb a rickety set of steps to an open box truck with narrow plank benches. The truck is jammed with people and there are nine of us to add. Yelling, pointing and jostling ensues as, one at a time, we are sandwiched in. Bob sits beside me, Lynda sits on his knee, and Simon sits on mine. Peter stands hanging onto the rail and Tristan and the rest of the troupe are standing at the back with the luggage piled behind them. It is hot and sticky and the truck must wait for the all clear before it can negotiate the steep switchback one-way road. Suddenly we are off. I grab Simon's arm to keep from falling back into the crowd, Lynda falls against Bob's chest. We are in near hysterics. In a bouncy roller-coaster ride, the diesel truck grinds its way up the mountain negotiating the switchback corners, climbing, climbing, and climbing for forty-five minutes of terror and laughter. In a moment of fear, Simon shouts, "Fuck!" and all of the locals turn, wide eyed, and smile, obviously understanding at least one English word. The little boy sitting next to Simon looks ready to vomit.

Arriving at middle base camp, we all stagger out into the crowd. Young boys carrying cone shaped baskets ask if they can tote our luggage up the hill. Men with sinewy, muscled legs offer to carry tourists up the hill in sedan chairs for fifteen dollars U.S. Four men carry the chairs on their shoulders. Thick bamboo poles with wide canvas strapping cradle a canvas and wooden beach chair, and the rider sits reclined with his feet out in front of him.

The journey is steep and twisty and made even more difficult by the stifling heat. The way is lined with small stands selling water and food. Elderly stooped women, wearing cheap plastic flip-flops, shuffle one step at a time up the grueling slope. Families with children carry enough supplies to camp for the night. Bare foot orange robed monks walk with their shaved heads bowed in prayer. The atmosphere is festive and the shops become more bizarre as we near the summit. Giant python skins lie amongst the wares. Stainless steel bowls hold putrid concoctions of centipedes, bits of meat, and deer heads impaled on sharp sticks. The offal from the gruesome stew is collected in the bottom of the bowl. It produces a liquid the colour of motor oil and it is rubbed onto the skin to soften it. One bowl holds eight small bear paws and a plastic jar holds tiger teeth.

Our hotel at the summit is simple and our back door opens onto a small balcony overlooking a spectacular haze covered verdant valley. Off to the right we get a sneak peak of the reason for which we made the pilgrimage, 'The Golden Rock', glistening in the afternoon sun.

I told Simon earlier today about a jeweler at the market who told me that you could pass a silk

The Golden Rock Pagoda

thread right under the huge golden monolith. Simon looked at me incredulous, "Excuse me," he said as he coughed, "Bullshit!" into his hand. Perhaps I had better not buy my ruby jewelry from that guy after all. Gullible as I am, I believed him!

After settling into our hotel rooms, we walk the short distance to get a close up view of the Golden Rock. An enormous head shaped rock topped with a golden *stupa*, it sits on a sloping block of granite defying gravity. A small causeway can be crossed to apply thin gold leaf to the holy icon, a sign warns, *'MEN ONLY'*. Underneath the rock, people kneel and bow in prayer and an unmistakable spirituality and sereneness permeates the air. A large hawk flutters his wings in the updrafts from the valley and the setting sun reflects from the golden face.

The next morning we are awakened by the monk's wake-up call, a four a.m. door knocking up and down the narrow hallway followed by monotone chants. After breakfast, we start a knee-jarring descent down to middle camp where we are once again jammed into an already over-full truck. Our local guide complains that he has to pay more for us because we take up too much space with our bloated western bodies. A tall thin man, wearing a leather hat and a longhi, sits stiffly next to me clutching a toy bamboo machine gun; it's barrel points up in the air. Is it a gift for a young son?

Tristan, Hendrick and Roger, are standing at the rear. Tristan has to straddle the honed edge of the tailgate as we head off on our downhill roller coaster ride. He is concerned that a big bump will compromise his ability to have children. We all pray to Buddha that the brakes on the truck are good. Bob points out signs at all the curves, in cryptic Burmese. We joke, "This one is called *'Dead Man's Curve'*." Tristan quips, "As long as we round *'Shit My Pants Curve'*, all is okay." The locals, not understanding our conversations, giggle at our hysterics and we laugh nervously as we careen around the hairpin turns.

The Train to Mandalay

The travel alarm rings at three-thirty a.m. This is the first morning that I have not wanted to crawl out from under the covers. In darkness, we are bused to a noisy train station. Tristan hands out our tickets.

The train was probably a jewel in its glory days. A castoff from the British in the forties, it has seen little attention since. Dilapidated and filthy, our coach has 'Upper Class' stenciled on it. Soiled lumpy seats are in a permanent, twisted, reclined position. Some of the windows are jammed half way open and smudged with a grimy opaque film.

At five a.m., the whistle blows the 'all aboard'. The diesel engine rumbles and as the train picks up speed, it settles into a rhythmic, *click, click, clickety clack, click, click, clickety clack.* The cars rock gently side to side as they dip and sway, dip and sway, dip and sway, a little like riding a galloping horse. The car is hot with little airflow. Our assigned seats are uncomfortable in their semi-reclined position so we decide to relocate to the dining car. It has small tables where we can sit and order food and beverages and a large open picture window to view the passing landscape.

Bob and I negotiate the tricky transfer from car to car; two steel plates shift side to side as the track races underneath. The countryside is dry and arid. We pass flooded rice paddies and farms dotted with giant cabbages. The echo roars as the train rumbles over trestles. Ancient oxen carts lumber down dusty rutted roads. These carts are from centuries past with five-foot wooden wheels, slatted plank beds, and pulled by oxen lashed to roughly hewn pole yokes. The beds of the wagons are piled high with hay, cabbages, tomatoes, and potatoes.

I love the train, a love affair from my childhood. We would ride the day car from Vancouver, BC to Winnipeg, Manitoba on my Father's free passes to visit aunts, uncles, and cousins. Even bracing myself to squat over the filthy toilet, as the ties pass under the open hole of the bowl, holds some strange appeal; the ever-present sign, *'Please Do not Flush While the Train is in the Station'.*

Most of our fifteen long hours of travel time are spent in the dining car with our travel companions, sharing life stories. As the train lurches to a stop at the Mandalay train station, we are no longer strangers.

The Moustache Brothers

On one of our evenings in Mandalay, Tristan asks who would like to go to the theatre. I have visions of a small theatre with a stage and perhaps some sort of a cultural show. I couldn't have been more mistaken.

After dinner, we wedge ourselves into the narrow seats of a trishaw; pedal bikes to which a rattletrap sidecar is attached. One passenger faces forward and one backward. The road becomes dark and bumpy with potholes as we near our destination.

'The Moustache Brothers' perform in their home. The stage sits street-side on a platform on the concrete floor of the garage. The audience sits one meter away in a single row of red plastic chairs.

The brothers perform satirical vaudeville skits full of political humor each and every evening. They will perform for an audience of one, if only one spectator shows up. They happily pose for pictures with audience members holding signs decrying, *'The Moustache Brothers are Under Surveillance', 'Most Wanted', 'KGB', 'CIA', 'CSIS/SISMI*, and a myriad of other acronyms and political statements. One large posted sign reads, *'Polygamy, Monogamy, Philosopher's Stone, Elixir, Herb, Root, Harem, Eunuch, Versatile All-Rounder Vaudeville'.* Their performance is kitschy, their English unintelligible. However, their message is crystal clear.

The Moustache Brothers

Why the Moustache Brothers are memorable is not their performance. It is the story behind their comedy troupe.

It is a family affair of brothers and sisters-in-law. Three brothers, the oldest Par Par Lay, then Lu Maw and Lu Zaw have been a roving theatre troupe for over three decades. They are comedians whose material contains much political satire in a country whose military leadership has no sense of humor.

In 1996, while performing at the home of Aung San Suu Kyi in Yangon, Lu Maw and Lu Zaw were arrested. Par Par Lay was at home in Mandalay at the time thus avoiding arrest.

Aung San Suu Kyi is a Burmese heroine who won the Nobel Peace Prize in 1991. She remained under house arrest for seven years after rejecting an offer of freedom if she agreed to leave Burma and withdraw from politics. Her sons Alexander and Kim accepted the peace prize for their mother in a ceremony in Oslo, Norway.

In 1992, while Suu Kyi was under house arrest, the National League for Democracy won an election by 82 percent of parliamentary seats. Suu Kyi led the party as general-secretary. The military established SLORC (State Law and Order Restoration Council) refused to recognize the results of the election.

In March of 1999, Suu Kyi's husband, Michael Aris died of prostate cancer in London. He asked the Burmese authorities to allow him to visit Suu Kyi one last time; however, his request was rejected. The last time Michael visited Suu Kyi was during a Christmas visit in 1995.

Lu Maw and Lu Zaw served five years of hard labour, of their seven-year sentence. They were released after high profile pressure from Amnesty International and several foreign comedians.

The government now turns a blind eye to their performances but the Moustache Brothers are always fearful and suspicious. Lu Zaw shows us a formal invitation to perform at the American Embassy, an invitation the brothers refused. "There may be video cameras hidden under the table," he explains. "If they want to see us, they will have to come here." He asks us to please pay our five-dollar 'donation' in American dollars. "The government made our currency valueless once," he explains, "people left with currency may as well have burned it."

Lu Zaw is the king of clichés and idioms. His English is so poor he often pauses to spell a word if he thinks we don't understand.

Following their performance, we buy cold beers to share with the brothers as we sit chatting.

As we part, Lu Zaw looks me directly in the eyes and suddenly becomes serious. Somberly he says, "You are my eyes and my voice. You are welcome anytime."

In a heartbeat, his mood shifts. "See you later alligator," he quips, a toothy grin splits his wrinkled mustachioed face. "In a while crocodile!" I snap back. The reality of the situation is that I will leave, and he will stay.

CHAPTER 14

Vancouver Island, BC – Canada

∞

Does a Bear Shit in the Woods?

September 2007, Bob and I embark on a strenuous adventure. We plan for nearly a year to hike the West Coast Trail with Bob's cousin, Daniel, and his wife Jody. Daniel and Jody are experienced hikers and outdoorsmen. They take long kayak trips each year requiring careful planning. They have to be able to read the weather and the tides and carry enough food and water to see them through both the expected and the unexpected. Bob and I would never have attempted the trek without them and their expertise.

When my son-in-law Jay heard we were planning on doing the trail he fretted to our daughter, "Michelle, I have some buddies who have done the trail. They say it is difficult and they are young and in shape. Your mom and dad need to train." Jay under-estimated just how stubborn and determined I can be.

When I was young, my father often told a joke about a bear and a rabbit shitting in the woods. Every time he told this silly joke, his face would break into a thin-lipped dog-toothed grin. Unfortunately, I inherited the exact same snaggle-toothed fangs. Dad had all of his teeth and most of his hair when he died. He believed in taking care of his teeth. "You only get one set of teeth in a lifetime," he would often say. He didn't take as good care of his liver; sadly, he died from cirrhosis at sixty-five. The joke went something like this: *A bear is taking a big shit in the woods when he notices a fluffy white rabbit beside him, also taking a shit. Turning, the bear says to the rabbit, "Mister Rabbit, when you take a shit in the woods, does the shit stick to your fur?" The rabbit replies, "Why no Mister bear, the shit doesn't stick to my fur when I'm taking a shit." The bear then reaches over, snatches up the rabbit in his paw, and wipes his ass with him.* I'm not sure just why Dad found this joke so amusing but he told it often and laughed every time.

The West Coast Trail is world famous, a 76-kilometer grueling slog through old growth rainforest skirting the west coast of Vancouver Island, British Columbia, Canada. It traverses several Indian reserves as well as black bear and cougar habitat. Hikers must pre-register up to three months in advance. The trail can be hiked from either end, starting in Bamfield or Port Renfrew. Only thirty hikers are allowed to start each day. Rain is almost guaranteed to fall at some point during the multi-day trek. The books say five to seven days are recommended. We took nine, and I needed every one of them!

The trail, hacked out of the wilderness to service a telegraph line between Cape Beale and Victoria, originated in 1889. In 1906, a ship, the Valencia missed the entrance to Puget Sound and crashed onto the rocks off the Canadian coast. One hundred and thirty-three souls were lost. In response to the tragedy, the Canadian government built Pachena Lighthouse and improved the trail to act as a life saving route for shipwreck victims and rescuers.

The following is an account of our trek. We were fortunate to see little rain during our nine days. I am convinced that had it rained the entire time, I should still be stuck in the quagmire. I have thought back many times over the past year about our adventure and continue to marvel at the fact that I was able to complete it. Often I say, "An adventure is a once in a lifetime." I can guarantee, unequivocally, I shall NEVER do this adventure again!

The West Coast Trail Chronicles

What have I gotten myself into this time? The backpacks are loaded; mine weighs in at thirty-eight pounds, plus or minus; Bob's weighs in at fifty pounds, plus or minus. Yikes! Bob has the tent and the food. Mine has, wait a minute, what DOES mine have? He is carrying the food AND the shelter, what else is there?

The trip was a year in the planning. If I remember correctly, it was a simple statement, "Someday I want to do the West Coast Trail." It fell carelessly out of my mouth after one too many glasses of Chardonnay. We were sitting on our deck in Gibsons, our tummies full. "Really? Me too! Let's do it!" Jody exclaimed. I should have called her the next day and said it was all a terrible mistake…but *NOOO*…now the time is here. I haven't slept in days. I awake at two or three a.m., my mind racing, packing, and repacking my backpack in my head. Did I pack enough food? Band-Aids? Socks? Great, I will start the journey exhausted, *AND* fifty-four!

Daniel brings his and Jody's packs to our house tonight. Jody and he will fly to Nanaimo on Vancouver Island by floatplane at two p.m. tomorrow. Jody's pack is thirty-eight pounds, Daniel's, fifty-eight pounds. *FIFTY-EIGHT POUNDS…ARE YOU CRAZY DANIEL?* We chat about tomorrow. Bob shows Daniel the slick tide graphs he has printed from his navigation system for the boat. Daniel talks about the need to be self-sufficient, the need for redundancy in our gear. "Um, for example, I always carry fire starter in my vest when I kayak." Daniel states. "If the kayak flips and I have to swim to shore, I can still light a fire." "If one of us falls in a creek on the trail and drowns, it will be unfortunate but the rest of us will still have our fire starter." *WHAT did HE just SAY!* You will call the Coast Guard to recover my body. Won't you Daniel? My head is spinning. I need some sleep.

The other night as I lie in bed, once again awake, my mind racing, I thought about our snack pack for our lunches and how you could really smell the smoky beef jerky. The odor permeated our packs. Wait a minute; if I can smell it, a bear will be able to sniff it a mile away! Great, now I have large, stalking, hairy beasts lurking in the bushes haunting my dreams. No sleep again tonight.

The day has arrived. We are on the eight-twenty a.m. ferry leaving Langdale, where we live on the Sunshine Coast. There is no turning back now. We have reserved the ten-forty a.m. ferry to Nanaimo on Vancouver Island. The weather is gorgeous!

We have lunch with Joe and Kim in Nanaimo (Bob's brother and sister-in-law) and meet up with Daniel and Jody around three p.m. On the road, we stop in the small town of Port Alberni for gas. Soon, we are bumping and weaving our way down a wide dusty logging road towards Bamfield, eighty-four Kilometers away. We swerve and dodge swift moving on-coming traffic, mostly pickup trucks. Our headlights are on. After we find what appears to be the town...Pub, Store, Campsite/Tourist Info... we quickly check the trailhead and look for a place to camp for the night. We set up in a camp, at Pachena Bay, on Indian land. The setting is spectacular. Waves lap on a flat sandy beach. The bay is a tight bowl with a small, scrubby, treed island at the entrance. Our site faces the ocean. A chunky driftwood blind protects us from the stiff wind blowing in off the water. There is nothing but open sea between Japan and us. After setting up our tents, we head to the Pub for dinner. Returning, we light a large, driftwood campfire to warm ourselves. The night is cold and damp with dew as we crawl into our tents. Unprepared for the damp chill, I shiver in my thin sleeping bag until my bladder forces me out of the tent. After my pee, I don my fleece jacket and feel a little toastier until dawn warms the tent.

Breakfast is pancakes with chocolate chips, maple syrup, and hot thick coffee. We pack up camp and head to the Pachena Bay trailhead. After our trail orientation, we arrange parking for the car in town. We are now waiting on the Government Dock for our water taxi, the Juan de Fuca Express, which will take us to Port Renfrew where we shall start the trail. Twelve-thirty p.m. arrives, no boat, one p.m.... one-thirty p.m.... still no boat. I finally call on the cell phone. "I'm just coming into the harbour," Brian, the captain of the Juan de Fuca Express says, "I'll be there in ten minutes."

Well, what a day! Brian is a true west coaster. After gassing up the boat, Brian slowly motors us out of the harbour. As soon as we clear the point he buries the throttles on the two 250 HP outboards hanging off the transom. Brian weaves us in and out of narrow passes littered with jagged half submerged rocks. The deep emerald of the water softens to milky sea foam green and then to a white froth as it surges back and forth over barely submerged rocks. The rocks are the reason our coast is referred to as, 'The Graveyard of the Pacific'. Brian eases us in to watch colonies of stellar sea lions basking in the sun. We smell their fishy odor long before we see them. Several enormous blubber rippled males stake their territories amongst the harems of females. As we approach, they bark and snarl as the females take headlong dives and frolic in the surf. The water is so clear that we can see them as they torpedo to the surface through ribbons of khaki bull kelp.

As we approach Port Renfrew, Brian offers to take us six miles off shore in search of whales. The surface of the sea is calm with giant undulating swells. We think for a while the trip off shore will be futile and we will see no whales, when, up ahead, Brian spots a humpback mother and calf. Brian follows them for about an hour and we watch, as they spray sun reflected rainbow mist high into the air. Reluctantly, we leave them as Brian beelines for Port Renfrew. On our journey in, we are suddenly surrounded by a huge pod of humpback whales. They spout all around us so close moist fishy whale breath permeates the air. What a wonderful way to begin our outdoor adventure. Brian deposits us on the dock in Port Renfrew. For ninety-nine dollars per person, today's whale of a *tale* trip is indeed, a bargain.

We camp in Port Renfrew, walking distance from the dock. After a glass of wine around a hot spark-spitting campfire, we slide into our sleeping bags in the tents.

Day 1 – Trailhead to Thrasher Cove
5 km

Luckily, we are able to catch a bus to the trailhead in the morning. Five dollars apiece, it is standing room only. A group of five women and one obnoxious man are also on the bus. They are taking the bus from Port Renfrew to Bamfield to start the trail at the opposite end. We are destined to cross paths with them somewhere on the trail. "Are you guiding the group?" I enquire of Mister Obnoxious, his muscles bulge in his too small t-shirt. "Well sort of," he replies, "They *ARE* all women you know," he states as if to answer my stupid question.

At the trailhead office in Bamfield, when we did our orientation, there was a sign reading *'72 Evacuations Since May 15/07'*. When we arrive at the trailhead office in Port Renfrew, one day later, the sign there reads *'76 Evacuations Since May 15/07'*. The fear factor is rising!

We sign in at the trailhead office, and catch the boat across the Gordon River. The water taxi across the river is short, and it deposits our trail companions, and the four of us, at the trailhead. We pose in front of the Pacific Rim sign for pictures. My pack weighs heavily on my shoulders; fear weighs heavily on my mind. It is time to start the climb, up, up, up a bumpy narrow path choked with twisted tree roots.

The day is grueling. We ascend and descend steep crudely made ladders on shaky legs. Passing over the highest point on the trail, we cross several bridges spanning mossy, fern filled streams. Giant old growth cedars tower above the younger forest, the thick canopy choking out the sun. We stop several times to rest our legs, allowing our senses to absorb the marvelous surroundings. A large guided group of ten started at the same time as we did, and we keep crossing and passing each other on the pathway. The day is long and unbelievably difficult. We do a lot of climbing, often grabbing roots to pull ourselves up and over. Daniel and Jody forge ahead of us and then wait for us to catch up, afraid to let us too far from sight. We play a never-ending game of tag with the group of ten. When we know the camp isn't far off, and the mob is gaining on us, we tell Daniel and Jody to go ahead, "Get us a good site," we say "we will be fine." We know the beach in Thrasher Cove, our first camp, is small and we will all be scrambling for the limited sites.

The last part of the trail into Thrasher is wet, muddy, and slippery. We are serenaded into camp by waves crashing on the rocky shore. The path down to the beach is a long series of crude, sloping, timber ladders. I am exhausted and daunted by the ladders. Jody waves up; a big grin splits her face. Daniel greets us as I step onto the pebble beach at the base of the ladder, "Can I carry your pack to camp for you?" he asks cautiously knowing how independent and stubborn I can be. *"YES. YES PLEASE!"* I beg. Jody hands me two thick slices of cheddar cheese, sustenance I desperately need. I stumble; tripping over thick logs lying like *'pick-up-sticks'* on the beach. My body is not accustomed to being relieved of the heavy pack and I feel like I am being propelled forward, pushed by a bully from behind! I keep looking back angrily over my shoulder but there is no bully to be seen.

Daniel and Jody have picked us the best spot. A double site tucked behind the logs in the shelter of the trees. I just want to fall on my face, but there is work to be done. We have to set up camp, and on the first night, it is our turn to cook dinner. Sorting through our food and juggling meals in either hand to determine their weight, we decide to start with our heaviest meal, the pasta. It turns out yummy, full of dehydrated mushrooms, sundried tomatoes, garlic, and spicy pepperoni.

I fall into an exhausted, body-weary, sleep, wondering how I can possibly don my backpack in the morning and take even a single step forward!

Day 2 – Thrasher Cove to Camper
8 km

We have to rise at five-thirty a.m. The tide must be low to round Owen Point. Several surge channels are impassable if the tide is too high. We start out along the boulder filled beach. The rocks get progressively larger. Some are bigger than cars. I tell Bob I now know the meaning of the verb '*to scrabble*'. Scrabbling is exactly what we are doing, over giant slippery rocks encrusted with giant jagged purple barnacles waiting like vampires to draw blood. Three times I slip and fall, lying helplessly in seaweed filled tide pools, flailing like an upside down turtle. Bob runs to my rescue time and time again, unceremoniously righting me and dragging me upright by the scruff of my neck. Again, we are playing tag with the crowd. They have turned out to be a lovely group guided by a company called Sea to Sky Adventures. The leader Mark and his partner Kelly are considerate of the fact that they are a large group and they turn themselves inside out so as not to intrude on the other campers. This is the fourth time Mark has guided a group this summer, an unbelievable feat, and he offers us valuable advice and info about the trail.

A young native park guardian named Stephan, whom we met on the trail yesterday, told us Owen Point is responsible for over eighty percent of the helicopter evacuations. "People slip and break legs or arms. Just go slow," he cautioned. Stephan is tall and lean with long, straight, shiny black hair, the colour of a raven, a shade and texture only seen on a full blood aboriginal. He wears black gumboots and a khaki park uniform. Sleeping in an old heavy canvas tent for the season, he assists the hikers whenever necessary. A large walkie-talkie is clipped to his belt giving him limited communication with both trailheads, in the event of an emergency. After cautioning us, he lopes down the uneven trail like a skittish buck deer, his raven hair flapping behind him like a black cape.

About three hours after we begin, we reach Owen Point and it is spectacular. The pounding surge has cut caves into the soft sandstone cliffs. The scenery is breathtaking. We linger for a short time taking photos, but decide not to push our luck with the tide.

Our travel companions on the Juan de Fuca Express the other day were a group of five Asians. When we met them on the boat, they had just exited the trail at Bamfield and were taking the boat back to Port Renfrew, where their vehicle was parked. They told us a harrowing tale about their experience at Owen Point. It seems that they thought that they had cleared the point. They were taking their time, taking photos when the tide, unexpectedly, caught them. By the time they realized their predicament they were in serious trouble. They had to be dragged by ropes up the cliff and over the rocks by fellow hikers, who realized the situation that they were in. All five of them had purple bruises and raw abrasions. The wounds, days later, looked like crusty toast and the bruises were still a deep blue not yet turning to yellow. They said they were lucky to have been rescued and extremely frightened by their experience. We want to take no such chances.

We decide to move on when we encounter a surge channel just beginning to flood. Removing our packs, we pass them up to Daniel who has climbed up ahead of us. We then sidle along a sandstone shelf before hoisting ourselves to safety. The rest of the beach walk is pleasant. The beach turns from behemoth boulders to a flat sandstone shelf filled with aquarium-like tide pools loaded with tiny fish, purple sea urchins, and lime green sea anemones. Giant blue mussels cling to underwater shelves. Three kilometers along the beach, we spot a jumble of floats marking *Beach Access 'A'*. After consulting our map, we rest, chat, and eat our snacks basking in the warming sun. We thought our gnarly day was through but we still need to walk a muddy trail full of broken boardwalks before reaching Camper Bay.

When we arrive at the river's edge, just before the camp, a cable car hangs over the boulder-strewn water. The river is shallow so we decide to wade across the icy stream. Bob takes his pack across and then comes to retrieve mine. Bless his heart!

Once again, Daniel and Jody snag us the best spot just off the beach and under the trees. Pine needles cushion our beds.

After we set up camp Bob and I wander out onto the sandstone point. Lying, hands linked behind my neck and basking in the late afternoon sun, the music of the surge serenades me as it floods and recedes into the narrow cuts in the sandstone. I am gloriously content.

Bob fishes off the point with a small casting rod.

Day 3 – Camper to Culite Creek
5km

We sleep late and spend the morning wandering the shelf and exploring the aquarium pools and cuts in the sandstone. Gooseneck barnacles hang on the steep walls. Purple sea urchins and green sea anemones take up residence in perfectly round honeycomb holes. The water, so clear and still, is invisible. We leave Camper about eleven-ten a.m. planning only to hike to Culite Cove. It is just five kilometers away but we know it will be five brutal kilometers. The path starts with a steep ladder and then quickly turns into roots and mud. We climb for about the first kilometer and then the trail levels somewhat. We slog through enormous pits of mud sinking halfway up our shins. Our knee-high waders save our boots from the muck and water. We gingerly navigate broken twisted boardwalks with large chunks missing. The boards, slimy with mud, are worn smooth by hundreds of pairs of hiking boots. Crossing deep gullies over flattened logs barely a foot wide, we inch ourselves across taking baby steps, concentrating and focusing on each movement, every flex, wobble, and sway. Crossing one boardwalk, it shifts side to side like a funhouse walkway. We finally feel like the end of the day is getting close when the ladders confront us! Steep long leaning timber ladders hug the vertical stone face of the cliffs. Slowly we descend step by careful step, down to small platforms with even longer ladders, waiting to tax our already wobbly legs. Once down into the valley, we cross over rickety bridges spanning streams just to face ladders towering up to the sky on the other side. A day filled with mud and ladders it has been exhausting! At Culite Creek, we turn toward the ocean and the crashing surf signals camp is near. We struggle on through mud and roots along the riverbank.

Daniel and Jody are making soup. The air is heavy with a cold fog rolling in off the sea. Exhausted, we let our packs slide off our shoulders onto a mossy log. Day three completed, we still have fifty-eight kilometers yet to go! Tomorrow should be our last day of the tough stuff. Yippee! Time to sleep.

Day 4 – Culite Creek to Walbran
5 km

Our last day of hell, we leave camp at Culite and walk the river to the base of the cable car. We decide to ford the shallow, rocky, river rather than attempt the cable car. Then it is up, up, and up the ladders, another day of ladders, mud holes, and boardwalks. These boardwalks are a pleasant change, wending endlessly through marshy swamps filled with purple-berried salal, yellow flowering skunk cabbage, and scrubby pine and fir trees dwarfed by an unforgiving environment. The sky is overcast and the temperature cool but not a drop of rain has fallen since we started the grueling journey. I kneel to the sun gods! I have a bounce in my step; the journey seems less demanding. Perhaps I am getting stronger.

The ladders are daunting. As I ascend a particularly long one, I count fifty-four steps, my age. Mud pits with twisted roots and gnarly fingers reach up to trip the hikers.

The highlight of the day is the suspension bridge over Logan Creek. With a deck about a foot wide, it is hung from thick steel cables pinned into the rock face on either side of the creek. Spanning

The Hellish Ladders

400 feet, it gently bounces and sways with each footstep. We reunite with Daniel and Jody at the bridge, posing for pictures, our cameras firmly clutched in our fists.

Logan Creek Suspension Bridge

More steep ladders face us, down to our camp for the night at Walbran. People we met earlier on the trail told tales of, "the nicest outhouses on the West Coast Trail." "New cedar ones," one fellow exclaimed. Well, they may be the nicest on the trail but they are certainly the most difficult to get to! Logs and tree roots block the precarious pathway. However, they do smell nice. Ah, the simple pleasures in life.

Tucked in the woods along the river, once again, we have the best sites. The river mouth is filled with squawking seagulls bathing and socializing in the fresh water. Backpacks shed we share Brie cheese, peanut butter, and crackers on the beach. Our campfire roars nearby. The sun burns through the gauzy fog and we bask in its warmth. I don my bathing suit for a dip in the chilly water and a much needed wash up. The nectar of life lures me into her icy clutches. I can never resist.

Just before dusk, we watch as a group of hikers arrives from the north. The river mouth is still deep with a high tide. The first to cross is none other than Mr. Obnoxious. He has stripped down to a black Speedo and is carrying his pack high above his head in the chest deep water. His female entourage trails behind him. As he passes us, he grumbles to Jody that we have taken the best two spots. He walks the beach back and forth in front of our fire and he stops with each pass to talk. His posturing screams out *"LOOK AT ME! AM I NOT SPECIAL?"* His chest is puffed out like one of the bathing sea gulls. Snickering, as do naughty schoolyard bullies, we secretly dub him Rambo, Mr. Wonderful, Superman, and Speedo Man. His weary harem sets up camp, in the sand, down the beach.

Ambling out to the point, we watch as a fireball sun extinguishes itself on the horizon. The waning sun floods the sky with reds, pinks and oranges brushing a watercolour on a soft blue canvas.

One of the women with Speedo Man stops us as we head back to our campfire. Speedo Man is crouching by the fire, his knees spread wide with a too small towel wrapped around his waist. He pokes in the fire with a stick. "How were the ropes at Owen Point?' she asks me. " Ropes? I don't remember any ropes. Oh yes, there was one pinned into the wall to use as a guideline on a short path. It was no problem." Rambo pipes in, "No, no, no, that is not what she is asking. We won't hit the tides right at Owen Point. I'm going to have to lower them, one at a time, down to the beach with a rope. That is what she is worried about." I stare, my jaw dropping, and to his female companion I say, "We made SURE we hit the tide right!"

Day 5 – Walbran to Cribs Creek
11.5 km

We leave Walbran about eight-thirty a.m. on a low tide hop-ing to cross the creek without us-ing the cable car and walk the ex-posed beach, rath-er than taking the forest trail. We gain time by walk-ing the sandstone shelf when we can, or sticking close to the waterline where the sand is hard packed. In

Resting at Chez Monique

some places, we have to walk in soft sand; the muscles in my calves and ankles cry out for mercy. The sun fails to burn through the heavy wet blanket of fog.

Just before Carmanah Point, we spot a roughly built beachside bar and restaurant. Chez Monique's, the much-anticipated promise of burgers and beer, burgers and beer, yeah! So near and yet, like a mirage in the desert, we wonder if it really exists as we drag our weary bodies along the never-ending beach.

A blue tarp strung taut over a pole structure shelters rusted tables and chairs. A young, scruffy, barefoot man stands in a kitchen area spreading burger buns with mustard and ketchup.

A sign on the wall reads:

```
Burgers    $ 12
Onions, Tomatoes, Lettuce
Bacon & Cheese Add    $ 2
Beer        $ 5
Chocolate Bars   $ 2
```

I order a fish burger and Bob a hamburger with bacon. Stacked high, huge chunks of fish fall off the edges of my bun. Glorious juices run down my wrists to my elbows as I stuff my mouth with the best food I have eaten for five days. The beer is icy cold and hikers, coming from both directions, are enjoying the camaraderie as they share their horror stories of, 'THE TRAIL'. We leave reluctantly, stuffed and sated, the first alcohol we have had for five days makes us feel heady and fatigued. Bob and Daniel stuff four beers into each of their packs as a treat for camp tonight. Loosening straps around our bellies to allow for the scrumptious lunch, we heft heavy packs onto tired shoulders.

A short walk through the woods and up a ladder or two, we arrive at Carmanah Point Lighthouse. The lighthouse was first built in 1910 although none of the original buildings remain. It is one of only twenty-seven remaining manned lighthouse stations on the British Columbia coast. We wander the grounds chatting with a young woman who grew up there and is now, herself, a lighthouse keeper. She is full of interesting information and she answers all of our questions. I notice that she is shy and uncomfortable and during our conversation, she never once looks us in the eyes. Her wristwatch beeps, signaling that it is time to report the weather to the Coast Guard and allowing her to offer her apologies and initiate her escape.

Leaving Carmanah, we walk an easy two kilometers, mostly along the beach, to Cribs Creek, setting up camp in a sandy patch behind a six-foot natural wall of sandstone. Surfer waves roll and crest in a continuous, calming rhythm. Bob lights an enormous bonfire attracting damp campers from the north side of the river. We circle around in the toasty glow sharing stories, and as our fronts warm, we rotisserie around to warm our frigid buttocks.

Day 6 – Cribs Creek to Tsuiat Point
14 km

We leave camp late with a long day ahead of us. Parting ways, we tell Daniel and Jody we will meet them at the Nitnat River where we have to cross the narrows by boat. News of a scrumptious salmon dinner, accompanied by an enormous baked potato, in the makeshift riverside restaurant has had us salivating since lunch yesterday. We start on the beach and we are able to stay on it for a long while, some walking on the sandstone ledge and some on the hard packed sand at the shoreline. We manage to stay on the beach until we reach Clo-oose where the Indian Reserve forces us inland. The trail then turns to mud and dilapidated slippery boardwalks. I have fallen a few times on the trail, always in the least likely places. Today I slip on a boardwalk and my pack throws me to the ground like a wrestler executing a half nelson. Bob comes running, "What can I do? Are you all right?" " Yes I'm okay," I growl. Just flip me over so I can get up!" " I can't believe you take it so well," he marvels. "Well the only alternative is to lie here and cry. Now help me get up!"

Upon reaching the Nitnat, we find Daniel and Jody sitting at a table on the dock playing crib, looking relaxed, as if they have been waiting there for hours.

Lunch is as superb as the southbound hikers promised, right down to the giant baked potato. After lunch, washed down with cold beer, our host, 'Hippie Doug', scoots us across the fast moving narrows in his aluminum skiff, which is fitted with a 115 HP outboard motor. Before he crosses to the dock, he rips through the rapids showing Daniel where the old trail entrance was located. Daniel hiked the trail twenty-five years earlier, without the aid of boardwalks or ladders; a monumental feat requiring ropes and climbing gear.

We still have five kilometers to camp and it is hard to get going with the big baked potato lying in a heavy lump in our bellies. Whyac, another Indian reserve, forces us inland once again. The trail is muddy, steep, and full of toe stubbing roots. Boardwalks are in ruins with broken and missing planks. We hike the beach route as much as possible arriving at a place called Hole in the Wall. The tide is just low enough; we can scale a couple of the sandstone cliffs, and dash through the 'Hole' on a receding wave. We are relieved when we find Daniel and Jody hidden behind a rock bluff, setting up camp. It has been a long day today and again, I feel like my stamina has been stretched to the limit.

The four of us have a nice private little site at Tsuiat Point until Pierre wanders around the bluff. Pierre joined our party the previous night, lured by Bob's roaring fire at Cribs Creek. The huge driftwood fire attracted most of the camp and we had a great time talking and sharing war stories with the other hikers.

Pierre is from Quebec and he tells all he has accidently left his stove behind in his van at the trailhead, a foolish and possibly fatal mistake. Pierre is a moocher. When he arrives at Tsuiat Point, he quickly stakes his territory for his tent and then sets up a clothesline between his hiking poles over our fire! He hangs six pairs of wet, dirty, smelly, hiking socks over it.

Daniel cooks a yummy scalloped potato dinner. He heaps huge helpings onto our plates. Angry at Pierre's lack of planning, Daniel stubbornly refuses to share. Pierre goes without dinner. After dinner, Bob and Daniel diligently cache our food in a tree. There is no aluminum bear cache in the camp, and a sign warns, *'Bear in Area'*. Jody frets because Pierre does not cache his food. Then, just before dark, she is relieved to see him wandering into the woods with his food sack in hand. As we turn in for the night, Pierre tells Daniel, "I hope it is okay man, I poached your rope." Daniel is furious at Pierre's nerve. Without asking, Pierre has lowered their food and hoisted his bag up using their rope! Daniel stews all night enraged at Pierre's brashness. In the morning, Daniel tells Pierre that he isn't welcome in our camp and he'd better move along. Pierre sheepishly responds to Daniel, "I hear you. I hear you man. I am going." We are on a cheesy episode of *'Survivor – West Coast Trail'*. Pierre has been voted out of camp without immunity!

Day 7 – Tsuiat point to Klanawa
4 km

As we pack up camp Jody has us laughing as she comically juggles three small white Styrofoam floats. The handle of her toothbrush juts from the side of her mouth. Playfully, Bob pitches one at her and she knocks it out of the park with her hiking pole.

Packed and ready to go, we walk a short one and a half kilometers along the beach to Tsuiat Falls. These falls are approximately two hundred feet wide and they cascade over a seventy-five foot cliff into a deep freshwater basin at the ocean's edge. Wide granite benches cut into the cliff divert the flow creating stepped vertical walls of water. I have seen taller waterfalls, but certainly none so dramatic.

The day is overcast and cool, but with a little encouragement from each other, Jody and I decide to take a plunge in the deep bone chilling pool. We cavort unabashed scrubbing away the dirt

Tsuait Falls

of the day. Sitting on a small ledge in the center of the falls, we let the cold-water pound on our tired shoulders enjoying an icy deep tissue massage. The boys light us a fire and we giggle as we dress, shivering until our pink skin prickles and warms. Back on the trail, up the ever-present ladders from the beach, we walk a narrow ledge and look down on the pounding surf. Rejuvenated, we walk crumbling boardwalks and cross a few mud pits but in no time, we find ourselves nearing camp at Klanawa River. A cable car sits suspended above the wide river. It is the last cable car on the trail. Daniel and Jody cross first stuffing their packs into the narrow aluminum car. Gravity zips them about three quarters of the way across and we pull from the platform helping them the rest of the way. Bob, whom I think is a little nervous at the prospect, and I, decide to send our packs first, a test run of sorts. Daniel pulls the packs onto the platform on the other side. Hand over hand, we retrieve the empty car and climb in. The car swings with our shifting weight as we zing along the thick steel cable. Bob grabs the rope to pull us the rest of the way and with Daniel's help, we are soon safely across.

Our camp is nice, at the edge of the river, in the forest. We build a warm fire on the beach and enjoy a quiet evening. Earlier, before dinner, Daniel tried his hand at fishing from the cable car high above the river. As the three of us watched, we questioned how he was planning on landing a fish, had he caught one. Perhaps, for Daniel, thinking ahead wasn't necessary. He was just a boy again, carefree and living in the moment, having fun.

Daniel & Jody Crossing the River in the Cable Car

Tonight it is my night to cook; my last dinner and the one I am most worried about being tasty - instant potato something. But I have a surprise up my sleeve. I improvise a dessert using leftover d e h y d r a t e d cherries and apples and a sprinkle of cinnamon. I spoon in brown sugar and a few All-Bran flakes turning it into a fruit crisp. The concoction is yummy, eliciting oohs, and aahs from everyone.

We are the only hikers in camp on this dark and spooky night. It is eerily quiet. Everyone is asleep. Lying in my sleeping bag, I feel the cherries starting to rumble, percolating like a septic tank in my tummy. Bob snores lightly beside me. My mummy style sleeping bag is cinched up around my head. Bob wakes up with a start, "Do you smell that? I think a bear just took a shit outside the tent!" His heart pounds as he scrambles to find the bear banger. I giggle. he admonishes. "He is right outside the tent. Can't you smell him?" It is all I can do to stop exploding with laughter. "Oh, sorry," I mumble sheepishly. "It must be the cherries."

Day 8 – Klanawa to Michigan creek
11 km

Our luck with the weather has run out. Through the night, we hear the *tick-tick-tick*, on the tent fly. Hunkering down, we hope it will stop. No, it sounds like someone throwing handfuls of pebbles at the tent. It is definitely raining. Damn it! We crawl out of our tents to a dull grey day. Bob's boots lie sideways and waterlogged in a puddle in the vestibule. Shoulders hunched, hoods up, we eat a hearty breakfast of hot oatmeal, huddled around the campfire. With stilted conversation we pack up our rain-heavy gear, and with rain dripping off our noses, we start down the beach.

The trail eventually forces us inland to maneuver the ever-present slippery-planked boardwalks. Many sections are askew or missing, victims of the past winter's violent windstorms. We are forced to slog through boot sucking mud pits with treacherous roots waiting to grab and trip. Parting ways, we plan to meet at the Darling River, the 14 KM mark, and the second to last camp on the trail before we complete. As we walk by a cave at Orange Juice Creek, a fire is burning outside the cave, but when we peak in, the occupants are not Daniel and Jody. Checking our map, we realize we still have a fair distance to go. When we arrive at Darling River, the camp is vacant. Where are Daniel and Jody? We check near the river, not there. We scope out the best site and lay down our packs. Bob has found a tarp on the beach and he strings it in the trees as a shelter, to keep us dry. Where are they? They are always way out in front of us. Maybe they took the forest trail and it was tougher, or maybe one of them is hurt. Becoming a little concerned, we question hikers arriving on both the beach route and the forest route. No one has seen them. What should we do? We decide we have no choice but to stay at our agreed meeting place. We ask hikers going on to Michigan Creek, two kilometers further, to look for them and tell them where we are. One young couple tells a fearsome tale about a bear that attacked a hiker in a tent, here at Darling River, two days ago. "He had no food in is tent," the girl laments. "Was he okay?" I ask, alarmed. The question unanswered, hangs suspended, one of the legends of the trail. Alone once more, we begin to chill. It is still raining and we have no fire starter, Daniel's rules of self-sufficiency echo in my head. Bob shaves a stick with his Swiss Army knife in a futile attempt to light a fire with a single piece of damp paper. Undefeated, Bob has the brilliant idea to use the flame from our camp stove as an accelerant. He is rifling through his pack under the trees when far off down the beach I spot a figure in a green jacket jogging towards us. "Bob," I yell, "I think I see Jody coming!" She waves arms high over her head as I wave back. Breathless, she tells us they decided to go on to Michigan Creek. They asked the guy in the cave at Orange Juice Creek to let us know that they may go on. He didn't, in spite of the fact that we had peaked into the cave looking for Daniel and Jody and paused in front of the cave to check our map. Nice guy eh? With relief, we drag our wet bodies into a private forest camp warmed by a sizzling fire. Daniel smiles, stoking the blaze with driftwood logs.

A wet dusk settles over the beach as hiker after hiker straggles in, forced to set up camp on the boulder-strewn beach.

Day 9 – Michigan Creek to Pachena Trailhead
12 km

Twelve kilometers left in our journey, today promises to be an easier day. We cross the river from our camp to a beach packed with the late arriving hikers from the previous night. The trail slopes up into the forest, steep and mucky. Long sections of wide flat pathways deteriorate into muddy pits with giant old growth timber blow downs. The past winter there have been some unusual windstorms on the west coast. In December of 2006, near hurricane force winds devastated Vancouver's world famous Stanley Park knocking down more than one thousand trees. The opening of the West Coast Trail had to be delayed several weeks due to the destruction. Some of the blow downs we have to scamper over and some of these fallen giants have thick chunks sawn out so that the trail can pass through creating crude fairytale portals.

Two kilometers in, we stop at Pachena Point Lighthouse for a visit and to wander the flowering groomed grounds. The lighthouse keeper's son is selling treats; chips, pop, homemade fudge (made by his proud and loving mother), to raise money for his college fund. I contemplate what form of culture shock he will face leaving the rock for college. The lighthouse keeper comes out to chat with us answering all our curious questions. He and his family have been stationed at lighthouses in various locations for ten years. It is difficult to imagine why anyone would choose to live such an isolated existence. As we chat, his watch beeps reminding him it is time to do his three-hour weather report to the Coast Guard.

Back on the trail, we count down the 'K' markers, 8K, 6K, Bridge 8, Bridge 7, Bridge 6… closer, closer, closer. *Holy shit, we ARE going to complete!*

Trail end. We made it!

At the 2K-trail marker Daniel and Jody sit eating their lunch snacks. We stop for a rest and when we resume, we stand aside to let them pass. "Uh, uh," Jody says shaking her head. "No way. We are going in together!" The trail refuses to let us off easily. We are almost at Kilometer '0' when we stand looking up an extremely long ladder. I count each agonizing tread as I drag my pack and my ass up the sixty-two rungs. Up, up, up we go and then along a short pathway only to face an equivalent down ladder! We trod on. The roof of the trailhead office peeks through the treetops. It is two p.m.; we have arrived.

We rejoice in our accomplishment, hugging and kissing each other in spite of the foul smell emanating from our unwashed bodies. Triumphantly, we pose for pictures at the trailhead office.

Bob catches the shuttle into Bamfield to retrieve the car. Back at the lot, we load our soggy packs, muddy boots, and gators into the back of the Jeep, planning to spend the night at the motel in Bamfield. When we arrive, we find out from the girl at the motel that the Pub is closed Mondays and Tuesdays. Shit! Jody and I both look at each other and simultaneously and say, "Lets drive to Alberni." Soon we are bouncing our way down the dusty washboard-logging road.

We all limp out of the Jeep dreaming of hot soapy baths. I didn't know that I could give off such a pungent feral smell; it is, frankly, frightening. After dinner and far too much wine, I collapse into a soft, dry bed, spiraling into a deep sleep.

The hike tested me physically, but more importantly, it tested me mentally. No crying or whining on the trail. I am thankful for the opportunity to become closer to Daniel and Jody, sharing stories of our childhood, our special relationships, our families, our travels and adventures, and our hopes and dreams. I love you both.

As to the trail, it's just a walk in the park...right! Oh and... don't eat the plump red berries!

CHAPTER 15

Malawi – Africa

Great Big African Adventure – Part One

Bob has an old friend Roger, whom I have never met. Both early risers, their relationship started over early morning coffees at the local A & W Restaurant in Maple Ridge. Bob and Roger are members of a brotherhood, a ragtag gang of cronies who have been meeting most workday mornings, for many years. Unlikely friends, they share their life stories with each other, but being men, they sometimes do this without even sharing their names. Some are young but most are old, with health problems, and occasionally after mornings of absence, they learn sadly that one of them has died, or has been forced screaming and kicking into a care home.

Roger is an Evangelical missionary. He fills Bob's head with stories of his numerous humanitarian missions to Brazil and Malawi. Bob and I have been to Africa once and Roger's stories of Malawi ignite a desire in Bob to return. The Dark Continent has captured our hearts and our souls in a way that we do not understand.

On our last trip to Africa, we met a woman in Zanzibar named Melody. She was on her vacation from Botswana where she is serving as a volunteer for Peace Corps in a remote health care clinic providing treatment for HIV/AIDS patients. We become fast friends and get to know one another over many meals together. She tells us about a website she is launching with a Canadian businessman whom she befriended when he passed through Nata on vacation. The website will raise monies for the clinic and the small village of Nata. Melody never once asks us for money but she enthralls us with her energy and enthusiasm for her project.

In March of 2008, Bob and I plan a return trip to Africa. We will spend the first ten days with Roger in Malawi to see the work he is doing, and then we will head to Botswana for a visit with Melody and an adventure beyond our wildest dreams.

We arrive in Malawi after two exhausting days of travel. Unfortunately, for the first time in all our years of travelling, our luggage fails to arrive with us. It is mayhem at the airport; we are not alone, many of our fellow travellers are also devoid of their checked luggage.

Before leaving home, Bob was a little concerned that I may not get along well with Roger. His concern however, is unfounded.

Roger is a complex character. He is extremely intelligent but curmudgeonly with a quick wit and a wry sense of humour. A man of contradictions, he speaks several languages but at times, he seems almost bumbling. He appears to be frugal, but then doesn't pre-negotiate his taxi fares. Gruff and crusty, but he has a marshmallow heart and cannot rebuff a street beggar. My heart warms to him immediately, he reminds me of my deceased father.

The luggage will not arrive until the day after tomorrow, necessitating our staying in the capital of Lilongwe longer than planned. Our accommodations are at a grungy, overpriced hotel called the Korea Gardens. The hotel is surprisingly busy, filled with missionaries and aid workers. I meet a woman in the parking lot of our hotel compound. She is warm and friendly and approaches me chatting, asking what we are doing in Malawi, the assumption being that few people find themselves in Malawi 'on vacation'. I have a stimulating conversation with her as Bob and Roger chat off to one side. Barbara is with World Vision doing fieldwork. She travels, checking the progress on some of their ongoing projects, rewarding work, which she obviously enjoys. Bob and Roger soon join our conversation. Roger asks my new friend Barbara, "Who are you here working with? Ah, yes, World Vision", he nods knowingly. "Yes, I saw all the new white vehicles arrive today." Roger states with a smirk. "I was blinded by the sun glinting off the gold cufflinks as your colleagues exited the SUVs." Barbara is unfazed and diplomatic in her response. She agrees that they do have their issues and she encourages Roger to complain those higher up. "Those types of complaints need to come from the public," she says. She points out that he is complaining to the wrong person. As the conversation whorls around us, Bob and I shift uncomfortably back and forth, trying to divert it to safer ground.

I must say that Barbara was delightful, someone I immediately liked. She talks about her two children, adopted from Cambodia when they were three and seven. They are now sixteen and twenty. Her daughter is at university in Toronto. She clutches a laptop to her chest; Roger notices the computer. Barbara politely states that IBM is on their board and they get them at cost, thank-you very much! To our great relief, we manage to ease them apart while the exchange is still reasonably civil.

The plane with our luggage is due to arrive from Johannesburg at two-fifteen in the afternoon the following day. We plan to be at the airport when it arrives and then get on the road for Ntcheu to hopefully, arrive before dark. Roger has hired a car and driver from Stanley, the manager of the Korea Gardens. It is a dinted and battered white Toyota station wagon with a cracked windshield and a teeth-jarring absence of shocks. After lunch we load up our carry-on luggage and head for the airport. At the turn off to the airport, we are stopped in a Police roadblock. As the officer approaches the car window our driver panics, "Say I am a friend. Do NOT say it is a car hire." The policeman questions the driver in Chichewa; he circles the car like a hyena scenting blood, shaking his head. Soon, the policeman and our driver are in a heated exchange. The officer pokes his head in the passenger window and barks at Roger, "Sir, who is the owner of this car!" "My friend Stanley from Korea Garden," is Roger's unfaltering reply. More harsh words are exchanged between the driver and the officer. Our driver gets out, opens the back of the car, and pulls out a dinted orange and black license plate with a broken corner. It is apparent that the plate is the issue. The driver, Charles, manages to jam the plate into place, securing it with one hex headed bolt. The cop demands a 1000 Kwacha fine (approximately seven American dollars). Now, Roger is furious, "Why was the license plate not put on at the hotel? I told Stanley I wanted no problems. He will have to pay for this!" The driver lamely argues that the police get paid little. Roger backs down, having made his point.

The plane from Johannesburg arrives on schedule. We watch it land from an open-air observation platform and then head downstairs to the airline counter. We soon realize that nothing is going to happen fast. "You cannot just go in and retrieve your missing bags. You will have to wait for the passengers to disembark the plane, retrieve their luggage and clear customs. The baggage masters must deal with the passengers from this flight who are also missing their luggage," the clerk curtly informs us.

Roger's anger begins bubbling to the surface once again. He badgers the customs officer standing guard at the door as he cranes his neck into the customs lounge to see if he can spot his missing suitcases. The officer stands firm; we will have to wait. Roger paces angrily lunging again and again at the customs officer like a pit bull on a chain too short. "Our bags are right there!" he exclaims in frustration. "We have been waiting two days for them." "I just want to get them and get out of here!" The officer stands firm. Finally, Roger breaks his chain, charges past him and beelines for the mounting pile of lost luggage. He retrieves his two large blue suitcases all the while motioning Bob and me into the lounge. The officer is still holding us at bay. Suddenly, Bob breaks loose and when I try to follow, he insists I remain behind. It is the officer's last feeble attempt to maintain some control. He will hold me hostage. As I watch, a customs officer rifles through Roger's suitcases, finally and reluctantly allowing him through. By the time Bob arrives at the counter with one heavy backpack slung over each shoulder the customs officer simply smiles and waves him through with a sympathetic, "Have a good day sir."

Back on the road, Roger continues to simmer in the front passenger seat. He is temporarily and uncharacteristically quiet. I settle back to relax and enjoy the three-hour drive to Ntcheu.

The countryside is stunning, a patchwork of lush valleys, endless plains and rocky jagged low-lying hills. The sun is sitting low in a baby blue sky dotted with white cotton clouds and as always, wherever you are in Africa, people are on the move. Along every roadside there is a deep narrow path beaten into the ochre soil by millions of tired feet, some clad in dusty shoes or boots but most bare, flat, cracked, and calloused. A few of the privileged, usually men in dusty rumpled threadbare suits, ride chipped heavy mountain bikes. Children and men alike walk hand in hand, a show of affection having no sexual connotation. The women, beasts of burden, balance water jugs, potato sacks, basins or stacks of twined together firewood atop their heads; their bundles haughtily defy gravity.

We arrive at the Angoni Beverley Hills Villa just as night envelops the land. James and Marian Logan will be our hosts for the next ten days.

'The Villa', as Roger calls it, is very basic accommodation. Our room has a double bed with the necessary mosquito net. An electric showerhead dribbles out barely warm water, presenting a constant threat of electrocution, in the small added on bathroom. At seven p.m., our hostess Marian and her staff serve us a tasty home-style dinner with an odd, sweet, green, avocado pudding for dessert.

Marian, Roger tells us, is an ex-nun and he considers her his right-hand here in Ntcheu.

Late morning, we head into town to the ECRAD office to connect with Pastor Manion. ECRAD is an acronym for Empowerment, Counseling, Relief, & Development, a Scottish charity that Roger works closely with in Malawi. Pastor Manion will drive us to the school in his 4 x 4 pickup truck. The truck was purchased from funds donated by the City of Trail in British Columbia, Canada. The vehicle has seen better days. Roger claims it was in immaculate condition when he purchased it just two years ago. The pastor has not cared well for the truck, and it rankles Roger. We bounce the seven kilometers down a red hard packed clay road finally arriving at the school. Children are everywhere. Barefoot and in dirty clothes, some wear tattered school uniforms. The school is red brick with a tin roof and concrete floors. It is well constructed but bulging at the seams with students. Having no desks, the children sit straight legged on the cold concrete floor filling the small classrooms wall to wall. There is no electricity and no indoor plumbing. Water is dispensed from the hand pump borehole well Roger drilled prior to building the school. There is no sign of books, pens, or pencils; no school supplies. Inside a classroom, I am suddenly claustrophobic, I feel faint, and I need air. I am on the verge of

bursting into tears. "Roger, why didn't you prepare me for this?" I implore. "I thought you were seasoned," was his terse reply. "I thought I was also but nothing could have prepared me for this."

Back outside I snap photos of the excited mob. The kids are thrilled to see their pictures on the digital camera screen. They giggle and point, not at themselves but at their friends. It occurs to me perhaps they have never seen a picture of themselves; do they recognize the face

Albino Boy – Poor Little White Lamb   smiling back at them; have they ever seen their own image in a mirror? One young boy, about ten years old, stands out in the throng. A baseball capped Albino, raw open lesions fester on a blanched face; yellow scouring pad fleece covers his pink scalp. He squints up at me, his pink eyes suspicious, poor little white lamb. I forlornly contemplate what his lifespan will be in the unforgiving environment. The hot African sun beats down. I am unaware that the tiny ghost of a boy will haunt my thoughts and my dreams for many, many months to follow.

Then there is Gerald. We wander over to a small open fronted brick building where two women are preparing lunch for the one hundred and thirty orphans Roger's society feeds. The women cook over a hot smoky open fire. A thick pasty maize porridge called nsima is the staple; a white bland lump devoid of nutrition it serves as filler. The women, along with a couple of the older girls, tag team stir the huge bubbling aluminum cauldron with thick wooden paddles as a choking smoke swirls around them. Orphans line up single file washing their hands with water as it is poured from a plastic pail. Each child is given a plate with a generous portion of nsima and a small scoop of 'relish'. The relish is the nutrition; stewed vegetables sometimes with a small amount of protein added; peanuts, fish, or chicken. The children pinch off a walnut sized lump of nsima, roll it in their palms, and dip it into the relish. They eat with their hands, no utensils. With not enough plates to go around, many of the children wait patiently for others to finish, rinse their plates in a slimy bucket of well water and pass the cleaned plate on to them.

In the hubbub, Gerald works the crowd. He is adorable and he knows it. A tiny, ebony imp with a cherub face, he is dressed in shiny yellow soccer shorts with a matching shirt. Gerald smiles on command, a big white toothy grin splits his face from side to side, inflating his chipmunk-like cheeks, and exposing tiny, perfect, white Chic-let teeth. He twists and spins disco dancing for our pleasure, his tiny bare feet disturbing the dry red earth. He is about the size of a two year old, the age of our smallest grandson. I have to pick him up, no; I have an overwhelming physical NEED to pick him up. He is uncertain as to my intentions, he grins from ear to ear, as I tuck him under my arm and heft him onto my hip. Gerald weighs nothing, stick arms and legs, a tight belly distended from poor nutrition. Wrapping his bony legs around my waist, he beams down at his buddies. I tickle him under his chin, clucking like a mother hen. He tickles himself under his chin, wanting more. I pinch his velvety soft cheeks planting a soft kiss or two. I instinctively rock back and forth. In the periphery, I hear the ignition of Pastor Manion's truck. It is time to leave. Reluctantly, I release my grip on Gerald.

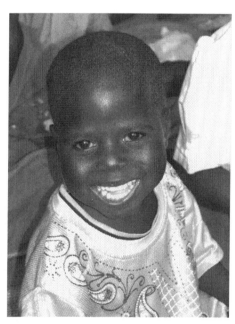

Gerald

Emotionally spent, I climb into the rear seat of the pastor's vehicle. "How old is Gerald?" I ask the pastor. I am shocked to the core when he replies, "Almost five."

Back in town, I talk to Bob, "We have to buy some school supplies." Shopping at a small well-stocked stationary store, for the sum of 40,000 Kwacha (approximately $280 American dollars) we buy one-thousand exercise books, one-thousand pencils, five-hundred BIC pens, ten pencil sharpeners, three boxes of white chalk, and two boxes of coloured chalk.

The day has been emotionally draining. As wonderful as what Roger has accomplished, it is a little like putting a Band-Aid on a hemorrhage.

The next morning, Pastor Manion arrives at ten-thirty a.m. to take us to the school. We load the boxes of school supplies into the canopy of the truck. Marian and the pastor's wife sit straight legged on foam cushions in the truck bed, nestled among the boxes of supplies. The road is slick from the overnight rains and the truck slips and falters threatening to stall in the sticky mud. Pastor Manion grinds the truck into four-wheel drive and I realize why the vehicle is in the shape it is.

The children are excited to see us arrive. The teachers welcome us and herd the children into the largest room of the school, they sing and clap as we enter. The room is filled wall to wall with tiny black faces. Their sweet voices reverberate from the cold concrete walls. The pastor announces that we have brought books and pencils for every student. The erupting roar causes my eyes to fill with tears. A swelling lump squeezes my chest and I struggle to suppress sobs. Bob, Roger, and I take armloads of books and fistfuls of pencils and pens and present them to the children one by one. The children sit politely on the floor with their hands cupped together, eyes cast up in anticipation as if in prayer. As they receive their gifts, they exit the school until we find ourselves alone in the cold hollow room. The school suddenly, has died.

Clancy

The following story is as I remember it, and from notes written in my journal shortly after it was told to me. I do not know if it is true, accurate, or historically correct.

While in Ntcheu, a barbecue is held in our honor. One of the guests at the barbecue is a man named Clancy. He is now retired, but for many years, he was a Malawian ambassador. He served terms in New York, USA, Edinburgh, Scotland, and he was posted in Cape Town, South Africa when Nelson Mandela was released from prison.

I like Clancy from the moment I meet him. He is impeccably dressed, his fingers long, slender and manicured. Tall and languid, he moves like liquid milk chocolate. His eyes are piercing and dark with spidery lashes. When he talks, you feel as if you are in the presence of royalty. The world suddenly blurs and all other sound is muted. The most striking feature about him however, is his laugh. Warm and melodic it bubbles easily to the surface and envelops you in warm, comfortable familiarity.

At the barbecue, Clancy slouches comfortably in a plastic lawn chair and chats with Bob and me. Clancy tells us that when Nelson Mandela was released from prison, he was stationed in South Africa. Clancy made it his personal mission to convince Mandela to visit Malawi. The president of Malawi, Dr. Banda, had co-operated and done business with the white South African government and because of this, Mandela vowed to never set foot on Malawian soil.

Clancy tells a story of Mandela's plane flying over Malawi to Mozambique when the pilot decided to land in Malawi to refuel. In flight, when Mandela was informed of the unscheduled stop, he raised such a ruckus that it forced the pilot to land in Zambia instead. Unfortunately, the Malawi airport had received news of the unscheduled stop and people were excitedly lined along the runway. The plane started to descend and then suddenly aborted the landing and flew off. It then became essential to Clancy, as Malawian ambassador to South Africa, to try to convince Mandela to visit. Malawi, being landlocked, needed a relationship with South Africa and Mozambique to access their ports. The future of Malawi was at risk.

Clancy went to Mandela's office in South Africa to request an audience. One of his presidential aides sat, feet up on his desk, smoking a fat cigar. He told Clancy that there was no way Mandela would agree to see him, but he would ask. To Clancy's amazement, he was told to return the following day.

The next day, as he makes his way down the hallway towards Mandela's office, he extends his hand to a minister he knows. The man shoves his hands deep into his pockets rebuking Clancy's gesture. Clancy is angered and embarrassed. The sting is soothed however when he walks into the president's office and is greeted with a warm hug from Nelson Mandela himself! Clancy explains to Mandela that Malawi was forced to co-operate with white South Africa to survive and asks him if he will please visit Malawi; it would mean so much to the people. He relays to Mandela that Malawi had allowed the black South African soldiers to don Malawian uniforms to pass through the country, during wartime maneuvers. Nelson Mandela agrees to come, but when Clancy reports the impending visit to his government, they refuse to believe him. Adamant, Clancy keeps saying, "It is true. He is coming." The Malawian government is so skeptical that the announcement of Mandela's impending visit is not made public until eight p.m. the evening before his arrival.

Before Clancy left Mandela's office on that fateful day, Nelson Mandela said, "Clancy, I have learned something here today and that is, to never judge a man before you have met him."

The Doctor

One of the other guests at the barbecue is a young Canadian doctor, Iona Haynes. She is in Malawi with her husband Michael and her two boys, Emerson, eight and Oliver, five. Iona is in Malawi with V.S.O. (Volunteer Services Organization), the Commonwealth countries' equivalent to Peace Corps. She is working at the hospital in Ntcheu on a two-year stint; she has been in Malawi for ten months. She graciously invites us to tour the hospital the following day.

Michael, who is content to be a 'Mr. Mom', is home-schooling the children but they also attend a local school. Iona feels it is important for them to experience the culture, engage local friends, and be part of the community. Emerson and Oliver are the only white children in attendance at their school. Emerson is in a class of ninety-four where three children share a desk. Oliver's classroom is devoid of desks.

The kids bring their own books and the school provides a pencil, which the children sharpen with a razor blade. Iona says, "It is indeed fortunate that their mother is a doctor." As part of their duties, the children are required to sweep and machete the grass in the school yard. Emerson has a scar, an old machete injury, on his shin, but Iona minimizes the seriousness of the wound, saying, "It was only a minor wound. These are the incidents we don't email home to Grandma."

Iona, Oliver, and Emerson have all had malaria in spite of the fact they are on the anti-malaria prophylactic Mefloquine. Oliver's fever came on so fast he had to be rushed to the hospital by ambulance, as he convulsed uncontrollably. He recovered fine, but scary stuff none-the-less.

The Hospital

In the morning, the hospital is bustling, and people are everywhere. We wander, eventually locating Iona. She welcomes us and takes us on a tour answering all of our queries.

The hospital has over four hundred beds and is habitually overcrowded. In between beds, mats fill the bare concrete floors to increase capacity. Dr. Haynes shows us the AIDS clinic, which sees one thousand patients each month. The number increases by fifty per month. We tour the lab, which has a T cell count machine waiting for a technician, and the x-ray department with a modern looking x-ray machine also broken and waiting for a tech (news to Dr. Haynes). A portable x-ray machine is being used in the interim. An ultra-sound machine has a probe that has been inoperable for over three years. The technician tells us the probe they are using works but gives inferior pictures.

Iona shows us the women and men's wards and the ward that she says bothers her most, the one she tries to avoid, pediatrics.

She says that when a child dies the women wash and wrap the tiny body in white linens, and then they roll the small bundle through the hallway on a gurney, wailing. Iona says, "I can't help thinking about how it would feel losing one of my own children. It is almost more than I can bear." Her eyes cloud and tear as she briefly loses her stoic resolve.

Iona is proud of the hospital. She says, "It functions well, considering what they have to work with." The operations are done by Medical Clinicians, not fully trained doctors but quasi-doctors who are trained in a three-year program. She says, "In spite of the training, they do a remarkable job. Most operations turn out okay, some not." I ask about the availability of medications, "Do you have anesthetics?" "Yes we have them," she responds, "however, they don't always use them."

The 'Operating Theatre' is out of bounds. It has a double swinging door with one cracked window that is held in place by internal wire mesh. A couple of the Medical Clinicians exit wearing long white lab coats, blue rubber gloves, and shiny white gumboots. I shudder to think what goes on behind those 'out of bounds' doors making white gumboots a necessary part of the standard attire.

Roots

Dinner tonight, we are invited to Clancy and Florence's. They live in a small modest home in town just behind a small convenience store they own. The house is concrete, nothing fancy, but ensconced in a compound of steel fences and gates nevertheless. The house is filled with dated furniture; overstuffed sofas, glass topped coffee tables with crocheted doilies, hutches and buffets crammed with knick-knacks and crystal; very fifties. Family photos, as well as political photo ops, fill the walls. Clancy and Florence are wealthy by African standards, but would be considered barely middle class in Canada.

The five of us, Roger, Marian, James, Bob, and I, arrive in James's Mercedes. Dinner is plentiful and delicious; chicken, squash, potatoes, beans, and coleslaw, served by one of several staff. A girl clears our plates and serves us dessert. Clancy pours red wine from a large green glass jug. The close friends talk money, family, and politics shaking their heads at the state of the country. They are warm and welcoming; we like them.

James drives us home squinting through the fogged windshield of the Mercedes. The night is dark and Marian nudges him, saving the car from dropping into a deep ditch, when he tries to turn into the drive too early.

The following day, James takes us on a long emotional journey back to his roots. He is offering Roger a five acre parcel of land near a town called Balaka on which to build a school, a piece of land which is part of his father's estate. James has not journeyed to his father's land for over three years.

The Mercedes flattens four-foot tall, golden wheat-like grass as it bounces down the rutted road. Nearing the homestead, the grass has been cut short with a machete. The road leads to a rusted wrought iron-gate. James honks. Roger offers to get out and open the gate. "No, there should be a boy here," James stops him. A muscular bare-chested young man jogs out of the house swinging open the gate. The compound is in shambles. James rages about his sister's children, "They are rubbish. They have vandalized the place stealing everything they could." I can see from the ruins that it was once a stately family home with well-tended gardens. Windows are broken or absent altogether, doors are missing. We enter the house to find the caretaker's wife. Through a missing door, I can see a cooking fire smoldering in the small courtyard. Two premature, malnourished, infants squirm listlessly on a straw mat lying on the cold concrete floor. The twins struggle to lift their tiny heads. The family is living in squalor. James shakes his head in despair, not for this family, but for himself. In the living room, a small showcase with a broken pane of glass holds yellowing invitations that are thumb tacked to corkboard. Invitations to university receptions, presidential receptions; 'RSVP please' 'Dr. Banda requests your presence'; an honored showcase of a time past, another era.

Exiting the house, we walk behind the crumbling home to a small fenced graveyard with four concrete crypts. James's mother, his first wife, and two sons are buried here. Both sons were killed in separate traffic accidents. James will be buried here along side of them; Marian, because she is a second wife, will not. Respectfully, we bow our heads in silence, allowing James a moment to compose himself.

James then takes us into his boyhood village, where his father was once the chief. An imposing cotton-candy pink Catholic Church sits at its centre. James says, "I would come to mass here until they made me angry." No explanation is forthcoming as to just what 'they' did. A young East Indian priest greets us. He welcomes us warmly, inviting us for lemonade. The parish is self-supporting. They have cows, pigs, chickens, and an orchard filled with fruit trees, avocado trees, cashew nut trees, and a healthy vegetable garden. Father John escorts us into a dining room and as we sip our lemonade, he blends ripe football-size avocados with sugar and rich, farm-fresh cream. He serves us the sweet buttery green pudding in chipped, mismatched bowls.

James shares a humorous story about his late father. He was in Lilongwe, working, when the police contacted him, "We are sorry to tell you Sir but your father has been struck by a car and he is dead." Grief stricken, James calls family and friends to report the devastating news. He then purchases a coffin and orders five cows slaughtered for the wake. People are mobilized; the word is out. A short time later, James arrives in the village with the coffin in tow to find his father sitting in the shade under cherry tree, drinking beer. "Father, what are you doing under the cherry tree drinking beer?" As an explanation, father replies, "My pension check has just arrived." "But father I was told you were dead." Spotting the coffin in the back of the truck, he ambles over saying, "Well son, and let's just see how well you did by me." Father, satisfied with the quality of the coffin, returns to the shade of the tree to finish his beer.

James keeps the coffin in the boy's quarters of his house for about a year, until one day, one of his sons comes to him and says, somewhat disturbed, "Father, sometimes Grandfather comes into the room at night and lies in the coffin." I guess he was test-driving it! James decides to donate the coffin to a needy family and his father lives happy and healthy for another ten years.

James takes us further into the village to his father's gravesite. His elderly 'second' mother lives in a small concrete shack near the grave. Polygamy is still practiced in Malawi. A husband is permitted to take multiple wives providing he can support them and the resulting families. We can tell by his 'second' mother's living conditions that she is not in James's favor although he greets her cordially, introducing us. James's father was chief in the village. A second grave of a manservant is close by. The manservant will see to the chief's needs on the 'other side'. I wonder to myself if the manservant was dead before burial or not, a chilling thought.

CHAPTER 16

Botswana, Zambia & Namibia – Africa

Great Big African Adventure – Part Two

Part two, of our 'Great Big African Adventure', takes us to Botswana. After seeing Roger off on his flight home, we fly from Malawi to Johannesburg, South Africa. We have pre-arranged the rental of a four-wheel drive camper unit, complete with all the necessities, fridge, dishes, pots, pans, braii (barbecue), chairs, table, and etcetera. Two collapsible canvas tents are mounted on the rooftop and accessed via folding aluminum ladders. Our plan is to drive to Botswana pick up Melody our Peace Corp friend, and head out on safari.

Our first destination is Moremi Game Reserve. We head for the city of Maun where we check in at the park office. Melody has reserved us a site at a camp called Third Bridge, deep in the park. The park officer tells us that there has been lots of rain, "The road is passable, but you must take the longer route to Third Bridge." In Maun, we stock up on provisions and fill the two extra jerry cans with diesel. The road to the south gate is washboard but decent. Melody's Setswana banter at the gate gives us a warm welcome and easy passage, "Dumella, eh, eh." Big grins split the faces of the sentries when they hear this pretty, blonde haired, white woman speaking their language.

The journey into the park has its challenges but park trucks have passed before us so we can follow, or not follow, in their tracks. Bob has had lots of 4 x 4 experience so my confidence level is high. We have one scary moment when we drop down into a deep muddy hole and stall. Bob pops us into four-wheel drive and as we crawl out of the hole, we notice an odd noise, a rattle. The road deteriorates and four-wheel is now a must. The noise worsens. Bob does a remarkable job bouncing us through deep slick pits. The once white truck now looks like a rhino, which has rolled in the mud. Just before we reach the first campsite at Xakanaxa, approximately four hours in, we spot several park workers. Just like men the world over, they can't resist a broken down vehicle and they come to check out our noise. The mechanic amongst them tells us that we have a hole in our CV boot. Bob knows that if the constant velocity joint fails, we will have no four-wheel drive, and it is a must in the park. The joint is part of the drive shaft and is covered by a gaiter or 'boot' to keep mud from contaminating the grease that lubricates the joint. We decide that we are best to park and camp at Xakanaxa for the night. Just as we pull into camp Bob feels a grind and we hear a pop; the CV joint has failed. Shit! We park under towering shade trees in a big open site at the river's edge and set up camp for the night. Tired, we decide to face our mechanical problems in the morning, in the light of day.

The next day we hire a flat-bottomed aluminum skiff with a 60 horsepower motor, to take us into the labyrinth of the Okavango delta, the largest inland delta in the world.

Melody chats with our boat captain BT. It turns out that Melody and BT have met each other and have acquaintances in common. BT plays an integral part in our eventual rescue. He offers to walk us over to Camp Moremi, a high-end, fly-in only safari camp. They have a mechanic on duty and a satellite phone. We talk to the camp managers about our predicament and they are sympathetic and offer to help in any way they can. Lance, the camp manager, attempts calling several times on the satellite phone trying to reach the camper rental in Johannesburg. Thirty-five dollars later, at seven dollars per minute, we have still not connected. Our choices limited, we decide to ask the camp to order the necessary parts. They agree to let Lucas, their busy mechanic, come after hours to do our repair. Camp Moremi radios Maun and orders the parts flown in on the morning plane.

Lucas arrives in the morning with bad news. The Nissan dealer in Maun quoted one hundred American dollars for the parts when the price should have been three hundred and eighty American dollars. The camp wouldn't order it without our permission. "Yes we need it, Lucas. Please tell them to order it." He radios camp and hopefully it will be on the one-fifteen p.m. plane. Three planes a day bring in guests and supplies.

Lucas returns with his tools and removes the broken parts in preparation. Later in the afternoon, after the plane's arrival, Lucas drives into camp with his head hanging. It seems the dealer has sent the CV joint without a new CV boot. The joint is useless without the boot.

Miracles do happen; the CV boot arrives on the five-fifteen p.m. plane. Lucas and his assistant Dix drive into camp with a newly assembled CV joint complete with boot. They toil into the night using the headlights of their vehicle to illuminate the repair, as they lie in the greasy dirt deftly wielding wrenches. We cannot thank Lucas, Dix, and Camp Moremi enough. Camp Moremi is a high-end camp and they could have easily said, "We would love to help, but sorry we cannot." Their generosity has saved our trip and we are eternally grateful.

Melody braiis us giant chunks of filet mignon over glowing wood coals. Creamy baked potatoes roasting in the flames for hours are slathered with butter to accompany the steaks and green beans stir-fried in olive oil. Melody's giraffe tablecloth is spread over our aluminum camp table and we pour cold white wine into our stainless steel goblets and toast our good fortune. Decadent.

Bob rousts me in the middle of the night. From high atop our canvas aerie, we peer out; a grey wall eclipses the moon. An elephant towers in front of us. He mills about unconcerned as he reaches his trunk high into the trees stripping branches of their tasty leaves and marula fruit. His coiled trunk then stuffs the tasty banquet into his mouth. An hour later, Bob pokes me again. A hippo the size of a Volkswagen Beetle is grazing between the river and us. As he forages, he emits deep resonating grunts. Lions roar in the distance.

Grateful to be mobile once again, our destination today is Third Bridge. The road has a few mucky pits but we are fortunate to be following a safari vehicle, familiar with the terrain. We convoy with a nice young German couple, Dani and Axel. Along the route, we pass elephants, giraffes, and herds of impala.

Third Bridge camp is infested with baboons, like fleas on a dog. The spot we have chosen is crawling with them. They bark down at us from the trees and screech insults when we try to shoo them away. They are so badly behaved that we decide to move to a site closer to Dani and Axel hoping that there will be safety in numbers; there are only the five of us in camp for the night. When Bob goes to move the truck, the baboons are all over it pulling on the straps for the tents and swinging off the radio antenna.

Dani is a sweet, petite, dark haired cutie. Axel is a hunk, a heart surgeon, in Germany. We like them immediately. Dani returns from a bath in the small river rubbing her hair dry with a towel. She encourages Melody and I to go bathe, "It is so nice, so refreshing," she coos. "Why didn't you shower in the ablution block?" I ask. "Oh no, I couldn't possibly do that. I am petrified of spiders." Melody and I grab our toiletries and head for the bridge. Third Bridge no longer exists; it is underwater, but underwater just enough we can use it as a platform for our bath. We step over a submerged aluminum sign with the warning, 'Danger Beware of Crocodiles.' Funny, I guess Dani has no fear of crocodiles. After a careful scan of our surroundings, we strip down unabashed and splash in the sweet cool water, giggling like naughty schoolgirls.

In our absence, mayhem ensues in camp. Axel has left in search of firewood. Bob hears an ear-piercing scream. Three baboons have entered the cab of Dani and Axels' truck through open windows. Dani, uncertain as to whether Axel has left the keys in the ignition, worries one of the baboons will steal them. She yells and screams waving her arms frantically trying to scare off the marauding troupe. Bouncing on the driver's seat, one of the baboons honks the horn and they scatter in all directions laughing like badly behaved teenagers.

At dusk, the entire troupe of baboons mills in the high wheat-like grass eating seeds and picking nits out of each others' fur; an idyllic bucolic picture of innocence. Babies cling to their mothers' backs and chests while adolescents tumble and play a

Our Safari Vehicle

game of simian tag. Adult males posture. The moment one of us turns our back, a thieving little hand grabs something off the table, out of a plastic bag, or from the back of the truck. Brats!

In the morning, we drink hot coffee by the campfire and watch as hippopotami bob and grunt in the reedy pond.

We decide to brave the shorter alternate road back to South Gate. A convoy of vehicles full of Italians arrived yesterday for lunch and they came in that way. They tell us, other than a few mucky patches, the road is passable. Fortunate, once again, we come across a high safari vehicle familiar with the area and by following; we are able to bypass several messy spots. Eventually the safari vehicle veers off the road into a camp and we are once again left to our own devices. Continuing onwards, we approach an ominous looking pit completely flooded with mucky water. We hesitate and debate which passage looks the safest, finally settling on a wide pass to the right where the grasses are matted and the water looks the least deep. Our decision proves disastrous. Tires spin and we sink. "This isn't good," Bob states the obvious. Futilely we spin and rock, spin and rock, spin and rock. Mud and rocks spray from the rear tires digging us in deeper. Bob opens his door, we are buried up to the floorboards, and water threatens to lap in. Damn it! In shorts and sandals, I open my door and wade out. Bob is in his hiking boots and long pants but he has no choice, he takes the plunge as well. He pulls out the shovel and starts to dig. Heavy mud matted with reedy grass is tight up to the under-carriage making digging impossible. Abandoning digging, Bob pulls the high-lift jack off the roof. He starts jacking at the lowest point on the rear bumper and it strains and buckles. The tire makes a deep sucking sound as it releases from the mud. Bob levers down one more time and there is a loud snap. The pin holding the jack handle has sheared off making the jack inoperable, stuck in place, and with no way to release it. Bob gives the side of the jack a couple of good boots, freeing it, but also cracking a chunk out of the taillight. I look heavenward and pray, "Thank God we purchased the expensive insurance."

Bob digs and digs and we are soon resigned to the fact that we will not be going anywhere without assistance. Collectively, we decide that if help does not arrive by three-thirty p.m., we will be forced to set up the tents where we sit and spend the night. It will be too dangerous to wait until dusk when the lions hunt. Cautiously, we gather the meager firewood in the area, fearful to venture too far. Lions and tigers and bears, oh my! Fire lit, we settle in for what could be a long wait. The tree shading us has one-inch deep claw marks striating the trunk from a leopard or lion stretching and marking his territory. A couple of planes buzz in the distance and every time the wind rustles the leaves of the trees, we think a vehicle is approaching. At two p.m., a large white Toyota Land Cruiser rounds the bend. The sun gleams off an electric winch on a beefy chrome bumper. "Halleluiah, we are saved!" Our savior is a big strapping Afrikaner dressed in khaki. His petite blonde wife sits in the passenger seat clutching a camera with a paparazzi zoom lens. The big South African positions his truck behind ours and instructs his missus to take pictures of the heroic rescue, our *White in Shining Armour*. Moments later, the wheels on the Land Cruiser spinning, his truck is stuck. He deposits his floor mat under the rear tire for traction and his wife in the driver's seat, and all four of us pushing, balls of mud spraying, we manage to free the tank-size vehicle. Bob hooks up our tow strap. For reasons unknown to us, the Afrikaner does not want to use his fancy winch. One tug and the rotted tow strap severs. Our rescuer finally agrees to unleash the winch and a firm tug nearly slices our rear bumper in half. Our truck doesn't move one centimeter. Defeat is not in the strapping Afrikaner's vocabulary. Now it has become personal. He repositions his truck on the opposite side of the swamp facing our truck, tying it to a tree for added strength. Holding a remote control, he pushes the button to activate the winch. The motor whines and strains, our front grill bends in half, the tree snaps. Our truck doesn't move one centimeter. Forced to admit defeat, the Afrikaner decides that he and his wife will continue to Third Bridge and return in the morning, hopefully with another truck. Perhaps with another truck and two winches, they will be able to pull us out. We are disheartened but at least relieved to know that someone is aware of our predicament.

Resigned to our fate, we are just about to set up the tents on the roof of the truck. Shovel in hand; Bob is trying to construct a dry base on which to rest the ladders when, along came John. A white Botswana 'good old boy', he immediately jumps out of his red 4 x 4 pickup and wades into the water up to his knees. John has a high-lift jack and is willing to help. One by one, Bob and John jack up the four corners of the truck, and with mud up to their armpits, they jam thick logs under each tire. Melody has

Our 'White in Shining Armour'

lost some faith in Bob and asks John to attempt the drive out. John is honorable and declines, refusing to step on Bob's ego. John shakes his head rebuffing Melody's request as Bob slips behind the wheel. None of us expects the truck to negotiate its way out of the mud on the first attempt. Bob and John know that they will have to repeat the process several times. Bob presses hard on the clutch and slides the gearshift into four-wheel drive low. Gripping the wheel in both hands, he eases down on the gas pedal slowly releasing the clutch. The truck shudders, the tires bounce on the slick logs, and Bob finds himself sitting high and dry on the far side of the swamp. Melody sprints through the mud following the truck with her arms waving high in the air cheering and screaming, "Woo hoo, woo hoo! That was just like a last minute winning touchdown at a football game!" She shakes her head in disbelief. We can hardly believe our good fortune; we will even have time to clear the park gate before dark. What the Afrikaner was unable to accomplish with his big fancy testosterone rig, Bob and John pulled off with a high lift jack and four logs. Amazing!

Days later we are in Nata at Melody's house, doing laundry. We will leave Melody at home and continue our 'Great Big African Adventure' on our own. Our plan is to head north out of Nata to Kasane to spend some time in Chobe Game Reserve and to visit Victoria Falls.

The road north is brutal, filled with deep potholes. We are eager to venture out on our own and along the way, we encounter elephants and giraffes as they amble across the roadway, nonchalantly, in front of us. Now *THIS* is Africa.

We reserve two nights at a camp called Ihaha, deep in the park, on the Chobe River. The camp has only nine sites and is *'foolly booked'* but we are given an overflow site just beyond the regular sites a little further up river. The site is private and secluded, cocooned by a small grove of trees. As we setup camp, a large herd of elephants bathe in the river just five hundred meters away.

We eat early, retiring to our rooftop perch at eight p.m. Nearing midnight, my sleep is disturbed by a need to pee. I prod Bob in the ribs to accompany me. Lions roar close by. Too close by. Quietly, we scurry down the ladder and I squat and pee in the dusty earth as Bob 'waters' the bushes. Five minutes after settling back into the tent, we hear them coming, tree branches cracking, deep chesty snorts, and trumpeting. The herd is right beside us. Our side tent flaps are down and the fact that we can't see them amplifies the noises we hear to a frightening level. We cower in the tent as six elephants pass directly in front of us, scared speechless as they nonchalantly amble through camp. A young male brings up the rear and he pauses briefly looking in our direction, his hind foot narrowly misses our still smoldering fire. As soon as the elephants pass, the lions start up again close behind us. Frightened by the night, I whimper to Bob, "What should we do?"

"What do you WANT to do?" he says. "I don't know. I'm scared. Do you think the lions will come into the tent?" I implore. "I don't know," Bob replies testily, "How should I know, I'm not a lion!" "Maybe we should get in the front of the truck," I whine. "Well,

The Lion King

you better decide fast!" Bob snaps. "They are almost here! The book says we should stay in our closed tent," Bob, feeling guilty for being brusque, gently reminds me. My heart is thumping. Will a heart attack kill me mercifully before the lions attack and devour us? Are we crazy? Our secluded little love nest, which we were so smug about discovering in the daylight, has suddenly turned into a terrifying, blood filled horror-movie. Stealthily, we descend the creaky aluminum ladder. We have to circle the truck to the driver's side, the ladder, and the tarp from the tent block the passenger side door. We sidle in the dark, like jumpers on a ledge, our backs to the vehicle, lunging quickly into the driver side door. Whew, we made it to safety. The seats reclined, we settle in for a long, uncomfortable, and fitful night.

The reservation system in the parks in Botswana sucks. They allow campers to reserve without payment for a limited number of sites. People book and then don't show up leaving campsites empty. It is frustrating. Two good sites sat empty last night and we could have, forgive the pun, 'Rested in Peace'. We decide we need a camp closer to civilization tonight.

In the evening, we head north and then out to a small point on the river. As we approach, we spot several giraffe in the distance. Settled facing the river with the engine quieted, we watch in amazement as a veritable Noah's menagerie ambles its way to the water's edge; herds of impala, buffalo, elephants, kudu, giraffe, and warthogs. I sit in awe, as the sky darkens to amber, watching families of elephants of all sizes as they wade into the river spraying cool muddy water across their backs with rubbery trunks. Bob dozes beside me, the sleepless night having taken its toll. I sit, smiling contentedly, contemplating the miracle laid before me.

Camp tonight is much more peaceful despite being cautioned by fellow campers, "Be extremely careful, there is a pride of lions just behind the ablution block."

In the morning, we pack up to travel to Livingstone in Zambia and the world famous Victoria Falls. We skip breakfast and head for the river to catch a ferry to cross us, and our vehicle, from the Botswana side of the river over to the Zambian side. We motor through town and as we approach the intersection, a semi-tractor trailer blocks the roadway, barring access to vehicles trying to approach from the Francistown/Nata road. People have told us to bypass the trucks. It seems that they are down to one ferry and they can load only a few of the big trucks for each crossing. After passing two miles of long haul trucks, we reach the border post to exit Botswana and our transit is seamless. We are confused. "Just go to the river," the Botswana customs agent says. At the river, there is chaos. Trucks are jammed together. Border runners approach us. "For twenty Rand we will help you cross the river." They will ease us through the process of crossing the Zambian border. We are suspicious - who are these guys? Well dressed, sleazy looking, carrying cell phones, they are especially persistent. We rebuff their assistance several times until we talk to a South African in front of us who is travelling with two young boys. He tells us, "They are necessary to expedite all of the paperwork on the Zambian side. They are worth the money. I am using them." Our vehicle is last, jammed into an uneven block of about ten. The ferry arrives and the first vehicle to board is a large overland tourist truck followed by a semi-tractor and trailer leaving room for only two small vehicles. Because we happen to be the last into the mess, we get boarded ahead of everyone else! We feel guilty, but fortunate. Hanging our heads sheepishly, we try to ignore the angry gestures directed our way as we roll onto the deck. Our border runner shadows us, following us on the ferry by foot.

On the Zambian side, our runner directs us to the immigration office while he runs to pay the ferry and our mandatory 200,000 Kwacha insurance. At the custom's cage we pay a fifty American dollar visa fee and fill in the book; name, license plate, vehicle make, vehicle model, chassis number, engine number, passport number, address, address in Zambia and finally signature. Then we move onto the next window. It is coffee time and the clerk is nowhere to be seen. Another book; name, license plate, vehicle make, vehicle model, chassis number, engine number, passport number, address, address in Zambia and finally signature, and then, another form to fill. We wait and wait. Our shadow returns and he takes us around the building to pay our carbon tax, handing us the 200,000 Kwacha fee. Paperwork finished, we drive through the border and park as instructed so that we can settle our bill with the runner. 200,000 Kwacha for insurance, 200,000 Kwacha for the ferry, 200,000 Kwacha for the carbon tax and 35,000 Kwacha for only God knows what, for a whopping sum of 635,000 Kwacha. The sum converts to about two hundred American dollars and does not include the one hundred American dollars it cost us for our visas. When the dust settled, I figure he ripped us off for about sixty American dollars but his services kept us from sitting in the ferry line for a week.

Mosi-oa-Tunya, the 'smoke that thunders', Victoria Falls is one of the 'Seven Wonders of the Natural World'. The falls are the largest in the world, based on a width of one mile and a height of three hundred and sixty feet. We hear them rumble all night from our campsite seven kilometers away.

The park has several trails and the first one takes us to the 'Knife Edge Bridge'. The end of the rainy season, Victoria Falls is swollen with water. Wearing our raingear, we walk over the bridge in a deluge of spray and marvel at the magnificence before us. Brilliant, primary hued rainbows spike skyward. Waves of snowy mist come and go allowing us stolen glances of the one hundred meter cascades. The morning sun beams around us conjuring surreal auras. The first tourists into the park, we explore in the thundering silence.

The next trail takes us towards a bridge used for bungee jumping. We realize at the trail end that we cannot get to the bridge without backtracking and crossing over the Zimbabwe border. Zimbabwe is in a political mess now, so we decide that getting closer to the bridge is not necessary. As we reach the end of the trail, a merchant selling copper bangles, wrapped in a greasy red rag, approaches us. He puts several of the bangles on my right wrist saying he needs money for food. The merchant is from Zimbabwe and he talks briefly about president Mugabe, and the election results pending. Bob notices he seems nervous, his hands tremble, he watches carefully over our shoulders, eyes darting. A deal is reached and I spin Bob around to get money out of his backpack. Our friend's agitation increases and he grabs the money from my hand and darts into the thick bushes, disappearing from view. Down the trail behind us, two soldiers approach. They are dressed in khaki and wear green berets and high topped worn leather army boots. Battered rifles are slung casually over their shoulders. "Who was that man you were talking to? Where did he go?" they demand. "Where did you come from?" "We walked up the trail," I stammer. "He was just telling us about the bungee bridge," I lie. We now realize our merchant friend has crossed the border illegally from Zimbabwe and we wonder what would have happened to him, had he been caught. Would he have been arrested? Or worse, shot in front of us? Our sympathy runs deep for him, and his country; the economy is so bad that their dollar has fallen to twenty five million to one American dollar.

My Flight with the Angels

I book a micro-light flight over Victoria Falls after listening enthralled to a young English couple who have just completed the ride. Bob will come and watch me, from the ground! No amount of coaxing will convince him to join me.

I am issued a navy, heavy canvas, one-piece jumpsuit. A full-face helmet and a headset with a microphone complete my ensemble. I kick off my sandals, going barefoot. I am afraid of loosing a shoe in flight, and it lodging in the propeller, plummeting us to earth like Icarus whose wings of wax melted when he flew too close to the sun. I am frightened beyond words. What was I thinking? I am terrified of small planes.

A single lap belt secures me into a tub-shaped plastic chair. The craft is an aluminum fuselage, shaped like a tricycle on

My Flight with the Angels

scooter wheels, with a triangular nylon kite. The engine is mounted behind me and has a caged, vertical, three-blade propeller whirling out of control. I straddle my young German pilot as if I am about to be released from a rodeo chute. There is no way this horse is going to buck me off. We bounce down the rutted runway at breakneck speed, the flimsy craft lifting off smoothly. Wind blasts against my helmet loosening it. We soar like an eagle out over the edge of the roaring, thunderous falls. I feel as if I am being held in the hands of God, total trust, total loss of control, guided by angels. I think this is how death will feel. We fly back and forth along the edge of the falls turning back over the wide Zambezi River. The pilot turns over the controls to me and I bank left to right, soaring on the updrafts. We cruise the river, animal spotting; two elephants, a small herd of semi-submerged hippos, and a crocodile looking huge, even from our sky-high vantage point.

Bob and I often say, "You can't go back." We have tried many times to re-live life changing moments but they always fail to deliver. My flight with the angels is one of those moments. I am sad that Bob wasn't with me.

On our return trip to Botswana, we decide to go via Namibia and the Caprivi Strip, a narrow strip of Namibia protruding east, bordered to the north by Angola and Zambia, and to the South by Botswana. By taking this route, we are able to avoid the ferry crossing, back into Botswana. We cross the border from Zambia into Namibia without issue, *stamp, stamp, stamp, stamp, and stamp.* Fill out the forms; fill in the book. We stop for lunch and groceries in a border town called Katima Muillo, en-route to our final destination, Etosha. A young Dutch couple we camped with near Victoria Falls told us Etosha was 'not to be missed'.

A long drive ahead of us, we hope to get as far as Popa Falls before dark. We are racing the sunset when we see a small sign for the community campsite listed in our newly purchased travel guide on Namibia. The small faded plywood sign reads '4 KM to Popa Falls'. Starting down a narrow deeply rutted sand track, we bounce through deep potholes as the bushes close around us. "This can't be good," I fret to Bob. A little roadside shack marked *'Reception' 'Honk for Attention'*, materializes out of nowhere. Our honks conjure up a wizened old gentleman wearing a ball cap and missing several front teeth. "We would like camping for the night please." "One hundred and twenty Namibian dollars for two," is his curt reply. "Go to site three." "Can we get firewood?" Bob queries. "Ten dollars more, go to site three, I will bring." *Okee dokee!* The sites are amazing, with a cemented rock fire pit, a roofed kitchen area, a double shower building, and a double toilet building. They are enormous but the best feature is how private they are. A little wooden deck overlooks the river and Popa Falls. Bob builds a roaring fire under the rusty hot water tank and we lounge with dewy glasses of white wine waiting for our warm fresh water showers. A blazing orange African sun extinguishes itself in the river. Alone in the world, in our intimate canvas roof top aerie, we drift into a contented slumber.

Honey, There is a Dog behind You

The morning is sublime; we eat greasy bacon and eggs for breakfast and then linger on our deck with coffee. Bob builds a blazing fire under the hot water boiler and I stand naked, in the sheer pleasure, letting warm water stream onto my face and over my rested body.

We spend the rest of the day travelling the long straight roads through the towns of Rundu and Grootfontien, to the park gate at Etosha. At four-thirty p.m., we pass through the gate and drive the twelve kilometers to Camp Namutoni, 'Disneyland Africa'. Camp Namutoni is not a camp but a resort replete with restaurant, gift shop, and pool. Wide lit boardwalks snake throughout the complex; one leads to a floodlit watering hole. The restaurant and gift shop are in a restored white-walled fort with a high walled deck overlooking a second watering hole.

We set up our tents and get the braii hot with briquettes to cook our tender filet mignon, smuggled surreptitiously through the Botswana border checkpoint. Seated in my chair facing the campfire, as darkness surrounds us, Bob says, "Honey, there is a dog behind you." Wait a minute. We are in a game park. There are *NO DOGS!* I spin in my chair to see not one, but several black backed jackals skulking within arm's reach. Scavengers of the night, the jackals have thin, pointed, fox-like faces, with slanted slits for eyes, a black button nose, and wide triangle ears. These canines are auburn in colour with a wide swath of black travelling the length of their back to the tip of a bushy tail. Sly opportunists, they wait for a chance to snatch our filet, and drag it off yipping triumphantly into the night. I don't think so!

Early morning, we game drive, spotting herds of plains animals, zebra, gemsbok, impala, wildebeest, and giraffe. On our slow, seventy-five kilometer drive to the second camp in the park, Camp Halali, we search for lions or a rhino but they remain elusive. Camp Halali, as opulent as Camp Namutoni, even has a gas station.

Our afternoon is spent lounging by the pool. Before dusk, we game drive to a nearby watering hole called Chudop, in search of lions. The usual suspects are there, a herd of zebras mill about, as well as a couple of wildebeests and a few impala. Bob positions the truck and totally engrossed, I snap off pictures of the zebra. "You do see the giraffe coming, don't you?" Bob questions. Five giraffe are heading down for water. Posing for my camera lens, stilted legs splayed wide, one lowers his cumbersome head to drink in a mirrored pool. We watch for about an hour and a half mesmerized by Noah's creatures. A small herd of wildebeests, some with small calves, slowly approach. Startled, a wildebeest on the periphery gives a deep grunt, a warning *huhg, huhg, huhg.* The giraffe raise their heads, and alerted by the nervous wildebeest, they lumber off on boney, stilted legs. The herd of zebra bolts sideways

A Perfect Reflection – Chudop Watering Hole - Etosha

in unison, sand flying from stampeding hooves. The object of the wildebeest's distress, a huge obviously pregnant hyena, skulks across the plain on a beeline for the oasis. The hyena, a pariah, drinks unaccompanied at the water's edge.

A watering hole or a location, teaming with game one day, can be completely devoid the next. It is all a matter of timing. This morning Chudop disappoints. We linger for a while, and then decide that it is time to head on our way. As we reach the junction, Bob turns, and spots several safari vehicles congregated on the main road. Curious, we turn their way and soon spot two young male lions making their way across the scrubby plain. They stop and tousle playfully in the golden grass, kittens wrestling. Getting up, one at a time, they saunter straight towards us crossing the road directly in front of our vehicle. It is thrilling to see the source of the chest rattling, hair-raising roaring that awakens us in our tent.

Elephant Toe Jam

We leave Etosha reluctantly, deciding to return to Melody's in Nata by travelling south through Chobe Park and Kasane. Crossing out of Namibia and into Botswana with little fuss, our only issue is with a heavyset, swaybacked Agricultural officer. She lumbers over to our truck wearing a long navy wool skirt, crisp white blouse, navy tam, and polished shiny leather shoes, her hair done in tight cornrows. The dowdy matron asks Bob to open the back of the truck and she rifles through the fridge. This time, we are not hiding beef we only have chicken. "She is thirsty," she says, pointing to a friend lounging on a grassy patch under a tree, at the edge of the road. We offer her two cold Coca-Colas. "She doesn't want Coke," she says nodding her head in the direction of her companion. "Okay, we will give you two cold beers then," I oblige. Officiously, she opens up one of the long aluminum drawers below the fridge. Two bottles of red wine roll back and forth. Her eyes widen, like she has caught us with contraband. "I want that bottle," she states bluntly. "Give me that. You give that to me." " We will give you two beer but you are not getting our wine!" I snap. Petulantly, she shakes her head and after instructing us to walk through the disinfecting bath, she accepts the two, proffered beer, reluctantly allowing us to continue on our way.

We enter Chobe through the Ngoma gate, hoping to camp at Ihaha tonight. As before, we are greeted with, "Sorry Madame, but Ihaha is *foolly* booked Madame." We pay our park fee and take the chance that we can talk our way into the campsite at Ihaha, twenty-five kilometers into the park.

The road, at this entrance, is a little worse than we expect and soon, we encounter a large herd of elephants. A gigantic bull stands sentry in the middle of the road; several elephants graze at the edge and we can see at least two tiny babies. Cute, little

Dumbo ears flap and their rubbery trunks twist to and fro. The bull ambles off to the opposite side of the herd swaying his head side to side in a threatening manner, his trunk dusting the road. Bob stops the truck, "What should I do?" My

Elephant in the Chobe River

sage advice, "I think you should back us up a little." The elephants continue on a path towards us, "back up a little more! We don't want to be between the bull and the rest of the herd," I state the obvious. In time, the bull plods across the road in front of us to join the rest of the herd. He pauses and stares, to let us know that HE is the one in charge of the situation. The lumbering pachyderms are still close to the edge of road. As we slowly ease past, the bull shakes his head, flaps his ears, and sways his trunk, stamping his feet in what we hope is a 'mock charge'. Without looking back, Bob stomps on the gas.

The attendant at the gate to Ihaha shakes her head, her eyes downcast. "We are *fooly* booked," she states firmly. This time the white board does look quite full of reservations but there are still three open spaces and it is nearing four p.m. "What about the reserve site?" I ask, knowing that these sites are available and she is not offering. "What reserve site?" she says testily. "The one past camp one. We stayed in it last time we were here." Reluctantly, she takes a red, dry erase pen and scribbles in our registration number. "One night only!" she snarls. In our naivety, we fail to realize that she is probably hoping for a bribe.

The night in Ihaha is uneventful except for one hell of a windstorm *rat-a-tat-tatting* our tent fly. The incessant noise was nearly as sleep disturbing as the elephants, hippos, and lions, which chased us into the cab of our truck the last time we camped at Ihaha.

It is time to travel back to Nata on the dreaded, potholed, Kasane to Nata road. Bob has slowed to eighty-five kilometers and he is doing his best to dodge the deep, teeth-jarring landmines, cruising along at a spot where the pockmarked tar is narrowed by tall grasses and bushes.

Have you ever been driving along, perhaps a little distracted, when a dog darts out in front of you, a near miss causing your heart to race? Now, imagine that it is not a dog darting out, but an elephant! Bob hits the binders locking up all four wheels. The truck rocks, fish tailing from side-to-side, tires squealing. The elephant, in a full gallop, veers right, away from us, his over-sized ears flapping hard like Disney's Dumbo, trying to get airborne. The look of fear in his dinner-plate size eyes mirrors ours. Had we collided, there is no doubt that we would not have survived; the truck flattened like a pancake, and us, 'elephant toe jam'.

The crisis passed, rendering us temporarily speechless, I turn to Bob and say, "I told you we should have redone our wills before we left for Africa."

Safely back at Melody's, at four in the afternoon, we are full of stories to tell as we gather around a small campfire in her yard.

Kgosi Maposa

Our day starts on a sad note. At four-forty five a.m., Melody's phone rings, a call from her father in the States. Her brother, fifty-nine, has died of a heart attack.

Melody has arranged a visit to a remote village called Maposa. We ask if she wants to cancel, but she insists that she will be fine, "It will be good for me," she says. She turns melancholy and is temporarily no longer there with us.

Maposa is a small village with a population of five hundred and forty. It lies on a sandy road seven kilometers off the highway and it has no electricity. Melody has chosen Maposa to be the recipient of our donation because of her fondness for the chief. Kgosi (chief) Maposa has invited her to the village several times encouraging her to talk to the children and to share her culture. He has never asked anything else of her, unlike most African men.

Our day in the village begins at nine a.m. Kgosi Maposa welcomes us warmly, a young man of thirty-seven and the chief of Maposa since he was twenty-six. A handsome man, with chiseled ebony features and straight square ivory teeth that sparkle from a perpetually warm smile, he is charming, slight of stature, but nevertheless, imposing. He takes us over to show us the school. The children are on break, so unfortunately, the school is lifeless. A small concrete foundation about fifteen feet by forty feet sits near the school. At one end of the foundation stands a crumbling red brick wall with a rusty iron pane-less window frame. The wall is part of the original school built by Kgosi's grandfather in 1954, left there to pay homage to his grandfather and to remind the children of how far they have come.

The new school is a well-constructed, long brick building with a concrete floor, but devoid of desks and supplies. Another building, 'the hostel', sits parallel to the school and houses one hundred and forty of the two hundred and ten children who attend. The hostel children come from cattle outposts, located over five kilometers from the village, and the dormitory serves as their home during the school year. The dormitory is divided in half, one side for the girls and one side for the boys. Both dorms are filled with rusting tubular bed frames topped with thin, worn, foam mattresses. A fuzzy acrylic blanket, the same blankets sold in markets of every third world country, covers the beds. At one end of the dorm sits a bank of dinted grey lockers, their doors standing ajar. Big tin washtubs nest beside the lockers, filled with wood fire heated water, they serve as bathtubs for the children.

I lean into Melody and whisper, "There is a real need for new mattresses here. Look how thin and tattered they are." Melody drags me back to reality, "You must remember Rosalie that it is a step up from what they are used to. The children sleep on mats on mud floors at home."

Next stop, on the tour, is the kitchen, a nice clean facility full of commercial grade stainless steel sinks and counter tops, propane cookers, tile floors, and stainless steel exhaust hoods; wisely wired in anticipation of electricity or solar power. A storage room bulges with sacks of maize and mealy meal. The 'hostel' children are fed three meals a day; the 'village' children are fed one.

The chief is deservedly proud of what the village has accomplished. The small village, devoid of industry, employed locals to construct a model school complex.

A reception is held at the Kgotla, an area under a large shade tree where tribal court is held. It is here where the chief deals with all legalities; disputes, debts, land rights, abuses, and marital problems. Red plastic chairs are set out and a white lace tablecloth covers a long head table. Children sit cross-legged under the tree as the adults congregate on the chairs. Melody, Bob, and I inflate and present balloons to the children. They stare blankly, letting the balloons fall into their laps, uncertain what to do with these strange orbs.

With the Children of Maposa – the vat of festering brew sits in the foreground on the right

Then the speeches start, a planned agenda of thanks and introductions. A wizened elder is called upon to verbally relay the history of Maposa Village. He wears a khaki jumpsuit; a broken zipper exposes a hairless chest and boney ribs. A cataract clouds one eye and his grin is toothless. Nervous fists worry a rolled, wide brimmed, felt hat. A village youth translates as the elder begins, "In 19, in 19, in 19...oh I forget!" He continues undaunted, "Kgosi Maposa (the grandfather of the current chief) went to the government requesting funds to build a school." The council said, "If we help you build a school, you will have to pay the teachers." And the chief said, "Eh." "If we help you build a school, you will have to buy the children books." And the chief said, "Eh." "So, it came to pass, a school was built in Maposa even before one was built in Nata, a much larger community."

After our history lesson a young senior student recites a powerful poem that he has written about the power of Africa, apartheid, and colonialism. A choir sings a' cappella tribal hymns as old gnarled feet and tiny bare feet stomp up puffs of sandy smoke. Women garbed in vibrant sarongs and headdresses, *yip, yelp, trill and kye-eye*, clapping to the beat.

As a gift, we brought seven hundred and fifty dollars' worth of sports equipment and school supplies, purchased in Francistown with donated funds from family and friends back home. We showcase the big items, the soccer balls, the volleyballs, the dry erase board, the softballs, and the aluminum bats. The children line up politely, single file. Arms outstretched, we give each of them an exercise book, onto which we pile, a ruler, a pen, a pencil, an eraser, a sucker, a bag of raisins, a bag of peanuts, and a balloon. When we present the school with the remaining items, the standard one (grade one) teacher stands up. A plump matron, dressed in a navy skirt and a crisp white blouse, her hair in long dark cornrow braids. She thanks us profusely for the large pencil sharpener, the kind we all used in school, screwed to the wall or windowsill, and operated by a hand crank. "For six years I have been sharpening pencils with a knife," she says, choking back tears, "for three years I borrowed a knife from a senior student, and when he left, I had to bring a knife from home." Such a simple gift, we wish that we had bought more of them.

Snacks of dried wild berries and mopane worms are passed our way. The caterpillar stage of an emperor moth, mopane worms are a delicacy, harvested once a year. The larvae, ten to twelve centimeters long, have bulging blue and lime green ridges with black feathery spikes. To gut the caterpillar, the body is squeezed between the thumb and forefinger, expelling the innards. The worms are then boiled, drained, salted, and left in the sun to dry to a crispy brown treat. Bob blanches at the thought of eating one of the caterpillars, but he isn't worried, he knows he can count on me to 'take one for the team'. They are crunchy, have an earthy taste, and are filled with protein, like peanuts!

Eating Mopane Worms

A cauldron of beer foams and festers in a cracked crockery vat imbedded in the sand to keep the noxious potion cool. Kgosi Maposa dips a coconut ladle into the bubbling brew and we bravely pass the vessel, gingerly sipping the sour concoction. A full traditional meal follows the snacks. A chicken was killed that morning; there is no refrigeration in the village.

More speeches follow, and then a casual mingling filled with intimate conversations. Bob bonds with Kgosi Maposa talking men stuff; solar systems, water pumps, electrical lines. He is surprised and amused when one of the men, attempting casual conversation says, "So, what do you think about that Dr. Phil?"

Like an old country picnic, the children bat their balloons to and fro in the background. Lingering until three-thirty in the afternoon, we part reluctantly after long goodbyes and traditional triple handshakes; handshake, thumbs up handshake, handshake followed by a soft touching of right shoulders, the Botswana version of a warm hug.

As we motor toward the highway, we pass children who enthusiastically wave notebooks and rulers, smiles warming their round faces.

Melody will leave Nata at the end of June after three years of service with Peace Corp. She has made many friends in Nata and they affectionately call her Neo (pronounced NeyO), meaning gift. A going away party is planned for June 7th and when she was asked what she wanted for a party, she said, "I want to have a big party and feed all the children. I have lived in your culture for three years and I want you to experience my culture, one where we value our children. The children will eat first, beginning with the smallest; this is what I want."

Melody will be missed in Nata. Whoever arrives in Nata, to pedal Melody's blue bike around town, will have mighty big shoes to fill.

Melody left with us the following Saturday. We dropped her at the bus station in Palapye, to begin a long journey home to the United States, to attend the funeral of her brother.

"Sala sentle Nata's Neo, sala sentle." "Stay well Nata's gift, stay well."

CHAPTER 17

Guatemala & Honduras – Central America

A Hand Up, Not a Hand Out

"Never doubt that a small group of thoughtful, committed citizens can change the world. Indeed it is the only thing that ever has."
- Margaret Mead

Bob and I volunteer for 'Habitat for Humanity' in our small town of Gibsons, BC. Although Canada is prosperous, there is still a need for affordable housing, and we believe in Habitat's credo, "A hand up, not a hand out." The recipients of Habitat homes need to qualify. The homes are usually offered to young families with an income, and the mortgage is tailored to their ability to repay.

It is because of our commitment to Habitat for Humanity that we decide to travel to Guatemala in the fall of 2007. The ten-day trip is not cheap. We have to pay our airfare to Guatemala, a fee to cover our living expenses, a generous donation to the Guatemalan affiliate, as well as cover our expenses for the *R & R* portion of the trip.

The airport in Guatemala City is new, clean and modern, and still under construction. We clear customs and follow the other passengers out of the terminal into a warm Guatemalan night. A throng of hotel signs and taxis await the unloading planes. Bob guards the luggage cart as I wander the sidewalk in search of a *'Habitat for Humanity'* sign. I see a man with a *'Crowne Plaza'* sign, the hotel at which we are staying. He speaks little English but he has a list with our names on it, so I am confident as we board the small bus. We discover later that the flight carrying some of the team from the west coast was delayed by fog and our team leaders assumed we were all on the same plane, thus failing to meet us at the airport. In spite of the glitch, we make our way to the hotel and connect with our team leaders, Ian and Paula.

The team, all Canadians, come from east to west with a singular purpose, to build small quality homes for poor Guatemalan families. Sara, from the Guatemala affiliate, briefs us in the morning. Sara is Canadian but she grew up in Guatemala and speaks Spanish fluently. We pile into two minivans for a one and a half hour trip to a small town, Guastatoya, near the build sites. Our packs and suitcases are strapped to the roof. The hotel is basic. Because we are a couple, Bob and I are assigned our own room with a private bathroom. The rooms surround a small well-tended swimming pool that will be a welcome respite when we arrive back dirty and sweaty after working all day.

In the afternoon at a welcoming ceremony, we are introduced to the families, which are all young with small children. One mother is eight months pregnant. She has a five-year-old boy with a shaved head and oversized ears. Another family has a four-month-old girl and a three-year-old boy. Mama is beautiful and Papa is extremely young. The third family has a three-year-old with perfect dark ringlets that cascade to her shoulders.

Everyone is dressed in his or her Sunday finest. They sit shyly at the back of the room and we sit at the front. One by one the women come forward, and through a translator, they thank us for coming to help. The men stand awkwardly at their sides and the children fidget.

The families must have income and supply the land, which is often part of a family compound. The total mortgage amounts to approximately three thousand American dollars and a payment system is worked out which is doable and affordable for the family. They are also required to spend five hundred hours of 'sweat equity', volunteering and assisting in the construction. These are proud people and it is extremely rare that a family fails to meet their obligations.

In the morning, two vans arrive to drive us to our build sites. Our driver Hugo is a stout and jolly man. Paula hands Hugo a music CD, a compilation of our favourite songs. "Musica Hugo?" One of my songs, 'The Cover of the Rolling Stone' by Dr. Hook, has the van hopping and we all sing along. I chose it because it flashes me back to my youth in the 60's.

We are split into teams of six and our team is assigned to the young family with the four-month-old daughter, Sofie, and the three-year-old son, Jorge. Thelma is a schoolteacher and her husband Gustav works in a bank. Thelma and her father work side-by-side with us all morning. *Abuelo* (grandfather) wheels rocks the size of footballs in a battered wheelbarrow. The work is difficult and the temperature hot and humid. Megan, one of our team, dubs it *'Habitat Boot Camp'*.

Each morning we are given a five-gallon jug of water and instructed to return it empty at the end of the day. Dehydration is a serious risk. The labour is all manual and the tools simple. Bob, Tim and the mason's assistant mix concrete on a pad. Six wheelbarrows of sand, two of gravel, and two bags of cement are mounded in a volcano. The cement rings the outside of the crater. Water is slowly added in the centre and the three of them fold and mix, fold and mix, fold and mix until it is a sloppy consistency. Then the bucket brigade springs into action. The rest of us, all women, schlep heavy buckets of wet cement to the mason. We also build rebar ladders to reinforce the foundation

175

and walls, hand cutting lengths of rebar and then bending them around a nail, on a jig, using a small specialized crow bar. The c-shaped brackets are then tie-wired to long lengths of bar to create reinforcing columns. Our hands blister, our backs ache, our muscles burn. We swoon in the relentless heat.

Lunch, the same each day, is two peanut butter and jam sandwiches on white bread, fresh fruit, a package of cookies, and a juice box. Some of us wear hospital scrubs that we purchased at our local thrift stores. For safety, we must wear long pants and steel-toed boots and the hospital scrubs are cool. At day's end, we shower in our filthy scrubs to wash them, donning them damp the next day.

Today is Canadian Thanksgiving and Paula and Ian have brought decorations from home for the supper table, napkins, a tablecloth, and paper turkey centerpieces. A can of cranberry sauce is doled out by the tablespoonful. It adds a festive flavour to my scant chicken neck and back. Our hostess serves us a sweet home-baked crumbly cake for dessert.

Within a couple of days, the foundation at our work site is complete and we start to lay bricks. Our mason Romero is impressed with his gringo crew and he is giving us more responsibility. He allows us to lay the bricks when he realizes that the women in our crew have a talent for it. Romero sets the corner blocks and strings a heavy fishing line corner to corner. Slapping mortar like icing onto the wall, he carefully places a block on the mortar and then with a hammer, *taps, taps, taps* it into place.

Laying Bricks - Habitat for Humanity Guatemala

Romero, circling from person to person inspecting our work, smiles a dimpled grin and winks when a block is perfectly set.

On the fourth day of our build, we have a serious medical emergency. Susan, a woman from one of the other teams becomes confused and disoriented. She babbles, attempting to speak Spanish, and she appears to be in shock. There are five nurses with us in Guatemala. Megan, one of the nurses, volunteers to accompany Susan back to the hotel. Susan is thin and frail. Sixty plus, she probably should not have been permitted on such a strenuous expedition. Susan spends the night in a clinic, on intravenous to rehydrate her. In the morning, she is transported by ambulance to a hospital in Guatemala City. Paula accompanies Susan in the ambulance and we are dismayed to realize that Paula will miss our closing ceremonies. All the women on the team promise Paula they will cry for her.

Today is a short workday. We spend the morning at the Quick Photo ordering photos for our Guatemalan families. Hugo picks us up and buses us to the build site of Ian's team. Red plastic chairs are set up in neat rows. Crepe paper streamers are strung in the trees and balloons hang in bunches like ripe grapes. A ten-piece brass band welcomes us, playing songs like 'Roll Out the Barrel' and 'When the Saints Go Marching In', on dull and dented saxophones, tubas, trumpets, and trombones. Speeches are translated from English to Spanish, and from Spanish to English. I speak, in Spanish, on behalf of the teams, *"Muchos gracias por recebienos en sus hogares y en sus corozones."* "Thank you for welcoming us into your homes and into your hearts."

The families give each of us small gifts, which they can ill afford. The teams present their masons and their helpers buckets decorated with ribbons, and filled with tools; levels, measuring tapes, marking pencils. I give Thelma a photo album filled with pictures of her family. She is thrilled and she passes it proudly amongst her friends.

A small boy from Ian's 'family' shifts back and forth nervously clutching a brightly wrapped package. He is the boy with the shaved head and the oversized ears. Jorge Mario, from the Habitat

Guatemala affiliate, explains that it is a special personal gift for Ian. Ian opens his gift and holds up a small hand stitched outfit. It belongs to the boy with the 'shaved head and the oversized ears', an outfit he has outgrown, and the only possession he has to give. Tears flow; a flood, with extra for Paula.

Sonia Eugenia is the mother of the boy with the 'shaved head and the oversized ears' and she is eight months pregnant.

In January of 2008, I received an email that embodied the following paragraph:

Ian Steven Luna Carcamo was born 20 November 2007 with a healthy birth weight of 8 pounds 10 ounces. Sonia Eugenia proudly proclaims that she kept her promise she had made to name her son after Ian, the leader of the group. As of January 2008, Ian Steven weighed 11 pounds and 8 ounces and was continuing to grow healthily. He is a happy baby who sleeps "a lot" and doesn't cry too often, says Sonia Eugenia, who has the support of all the neighborhood families and little girls to help take care of him.

As we depart in the van, Kit turns to me choking back tears. "*They* just don't realize how much *they* have given *us*!"

Isles de Bahia, Honduras

Following the build, we leave the Habitat team in Antigua, Guatemala, spend some time exploring, and eventually find our way through Honduras to complete our adventure with some underwater *R & R* on Roatan. The island has been a Mecca for divers for years, heavily featured in all of the scuba diving magazines. Outside of the diving community, it is little known.

We fall in love with the funky little island within the first couple of days. Holding hands like newlyweds, Bob and I walk the beaches for hours. At dusk, clinking dewy wine glasses, we watch as the orange Caribbean sun slips into the sea. Walks take us down the sandy potholed road through West End and we lunch daily at different open-air restaurants. Tropical rainstorms drench us unexpectedly and we take pleasure in their warm and steamy wetness.

One afternoon, as we walk along the beach from West Bay to West End, we pass a dive shop perched over the ocean. The dive master in the shop stops us, "Where in Canada are you guys from?" Once again, Bob's 'Canada' ball cap, has introduced us to a new friend. Bob proffers the usual reply, "Near Vancouver." "Where, near Vancouver?" "Gibsons," Bob says. "Hey, I am from Kelowna. My wife Lisa and I sold everything and moved down here three years ago. We bought ten acres in Camp Bay."

Stuart, tattooed, tall, and lean with a shaven head, which he often covers with a printed cotton skullcap, was a fireman in Kelowna, British Columbia. He reminds me of my son Bobby who is also a fireman. He carries himself with a bad boy swagger, which couldn't be farther from the truth. I like him immediately. We chat for a long time. "Yeah, Lisa is selling real estate on the island. We love it here," Stuart says. We talk until we realize the dark is going to catch us and we have some rocky shore to navigate on our way back to Luna Beach Resort. Holding hands, Bob and I talk as we walk, "maybe we should go back tomorrow and tell Stuart we would like to meet Lisa and see what is for sale here," I gently suggest. "You never know, it could be a good investment and we could afford to get into something right now." "Sure, why not, it doesn't cost us anything to look," Bob replies. Little did he know how wrong that statement would prove to be.

CHAPTER 18

Roatan, Honduras – Central America

Casa Rosalia

In November of 2008, we travel to the tropical island of Roatan, Honduras. Smitten by the emerald and aqua jewel, we are on a house hunting mission. White sugar beaches dot the shoreline like a milky strand of pearls encircling the throat of a princess. We return to Roatan to see if the passion was simply a holiday fling or if it is to be a lasting relationship. "We have to go back and either buy a house or get it out of our system," I declare to Bob.

We find our home in Sandy Bay, near the west end of the island, and it is spectacular. Perched high on a ridge, it overlooks the azure sea, and the dolphin pens of Anthony's Key Resort. The resort is a high-end all-inclusive dive resort. In the afternoon, we watch as cruise ship passengers and tourists stand knee deep in the lagoon interacting with the resort's twenty plus, captive, bottle-nosed dolphins.

Our gardens are immaculate, carefully tended by Juven, our gardener/watchman. Banana trees, papaya trees, guava trees, palm trees, and a plethora of blooming tropical plants dot the slope. Emerald hummingbirds extract nectar from red and yellow blossoms. Vibrant lime green geckos scurry along the white Grecian columns and walls of our villa. Trade winds sway the palm fronds providing a welcome relief from the tropical sun. We have found our Nirvana!

I Told You That Driveway Was Steep!

Possession date for our casa is January 19, 2009. Arriving on January 17th, we plan on spending a couple of days at a little 'boutique' resort, called the Blue Bahia. Unfortunately, *NOTHING* happens on schedule in Honduras.

The real estate purchasing process in Honduras is not for the faint of heart. We are confident in our real estate agent and in our Honduran lawyer; however, we spend three extremely stress-filled days beyond our closing and possession date waiting for the myriad of complications to be ironed out.

January 21st, all the papers are signed and the house is finally ours.

One of the few drawbacks of our heavenly aerie nest is the wickedly steep driveway. Constructed of deeply ridged concrete, the angle is brutal to walk up and impossible to walk down. A slick layer of algae, when wet, creates a life threatening descent.

A couple of days after moving in, we decide it is time to walk over and greet our neighbor. He is an Italian, named Rocco, and rumor has it there was a strained relationship between him and the previous owners of our house, an American couple from Portland, Oregon. We suspect Rocco is responsible for some of the snags encountered during our purchasing process and we feel it is important to start out on good terms.

Rocco is a large imposing man, serious, with an arrogant air. We paste on our best 'howdy neighbor' smiles in an attempt to disarm him. He is cautious, and a little suspicious, but friendly enough, even inviting us in for a cup of coffee. We decline coffee, chatting on his porch step.

Our pickup truck is being repaired and we have a rental car we cannot get up the driveway, so we have been parking it at the neighbor below; the house is empty. The house belongs to a friend of Rocco's so we assure him that we will have our 4x4 truck back from the mechanic soon and the car will then be gone. "You do know what happened to your truck. Don't you?" Rocco asks. "No. What?" Bob responds. "Well, they brought the refrigerator up to the top of the driveway and when they removed it from the box of the truck, it took the weight off the back wheels. Unoccupied, the truck rolled out of the carport, hit the concrete wall, and flipped upside down like a pizza onto the delivery truck at the bottom of the bank!" The bank is approximately fifty feet high.

Later, when we tell our mechanic he laughs, "That explains it! I knew your truck had been in an accident."

The R.E.C.O. Protest

In November, the week prior to us arriving in Roatan to house hunt, there was a serious protest. Giant diesel generators, in all manner of disrepair, provide electricity for the island. Housed in rusting wheeled boxcars with open doors for ventilation, black grease oozes from them as they noisily belch acrid diesel fumes.

The electric company R.E.C.O. (Roatan Electric Company) was on the verge of bankruptcy and bought by an American conglomerate owned by a Texan billionaire named Kelcy Warren. As soon as the American company took over, they doubled the rates. The move was probably necessary, the too low rates causing the financial problems of the predecessor. However, Honduras is a poor country and the sudden and drastic rate increase, did not sit well with the locals.

On November 5th, blockades were set up at strategic points around the island. For two days, residents, locals and ex-pats alike, were held hostage in their homes. Rumor has it that many of the protestors were ferried over from the mainland: paid protestors. Fires were lit, thick logs dragged across the roadways, machetes waved in the air, and firearms brandished. No one dared to challenge the angry mob.

The protest paralyzed the island. Two cruise ships would not dock at the Cruise Ship Terminal on Wednesday and the companies threatened to eliminate Roatan as a port of call if any future protests occurred. Electricity was cut to the entire island. The Airport was shut down, no flights in or out. The United States government issued a travel advisory. The financial impact reverberated across the island.

There is a high-end furniture store on the island called Atocha. It is located in the ex-pat community of French Harbour, and owned by a Spaniard named Santana. Santana is as slick and smooth as any used car salesman; young, energetic, and handsome in a smarmy way. While living with his young family in San Pedro Sula, on the mainland of Honduras, he would offer his services to the ex-pats on Roatan. Santana would shop in San Pedro and arrange shipping to the island on the freight boat, for a small fee. Business was good; he was trusted and respected. Servicing his customers well, he often secured prices far below those that they could arrange themselves.

San Pedro, where he and his family lived, was dangerous. His vehicle was chased twice at high speeds by would be armed robbers. He feared for the safety of his young family, a wife, and three small boys. His wife, Fatima, did not want to leave San Pedro and move to Roatan. Her family lived in San Pedro, as well as all of her friends. Santana commuted back and forth for months before finally convincing her that they could live well in Roatan, open their own furniture business, and the children would be safer there. Fatima relented when he found a nice house for them to rent. The landlord promised to complete it for them; it still needed work; drywall, tile floors, plumbing. Three months later, the landlord had done none of the renovations so Santana offered to complete them himself. The landlord agreed to take the expense off rent due.

Happy, the house completed, Santana moved his lovely family to Roatan, as well as his Mother, Mercedes. She would help in the furniture store, allowing Santana more time with his customers and Fatima the time to stay at home with their three young boys.

The day they moved into their rental house, the water was not working. Fatima, with a six-month-old baby was not amused. Santana investigated and discovered that the neighbor above them had cut off their water pipe. Santana is a Spaniard and the neighbor was not about to welcome them. Santana went to his landlord and said, "You better get this fixed. I have spent nine thousand dollars finishing the house and now my wife wants to go back to San Pedro!" The landlord was able to quickly remedy the situation much to Santana's relief.

Then the R.E.C.O. protest happened.

Santana and Fatima's six-month-old son has several allergies. He is glucose and lactose intolerant as well as having other issues and he requires special formula. They were down to one bottle and the new supply of formula was at the airport, behind the blockades. Santana headed for the door and Fatima, alarmed, inquired, "Where are you going?" "I am going to the airport to get the milk for the baby!"

Crazed, Santana jumped into his four-wheel drive SUV and drove like a wild man until he reached the blockade. He leapt out in defiance and confronted the angry protestors. "I jumped out with my 12 gauge across my chest and I said, my son needs milk and either you let me through or *I AM GOING THROUGH!*" The protesters wisely allowed him passage but he had to park far from the airport and walk the gauntlet of protestors in and out.

Two days later it was all over and the island settled back to an idyllic paradise. We arrive the following Saturday, unaware of all of the excitement we had missed.

CHAPTER 19

Malawi – Africa

A Special Journey

The Boileau family was struck by tragedy in August of 2008. Bob's brother Dennis's son, Troy, was doing some tree trimming for his sister-in-law and brother-in law. Troy's wife, Cindy, was thrilled when her sister and her husband moved onto rural property just a few doors down. They would be neighbors and Cindy, being a stay at home mom, was looking forward to spending more time with her sister Lori and her family.

It was the weekend and Troy was balanced on a three-legged aluminum orchard ladder just finishing up for the day. Cindy said her goodbyes to her sister and stopped at the bottom of the ladder to tell Troy that she was going home to start dinner and she would see him there. He never made it home. Troy fell from the ladder hitting his head on a concrete curb. First on scene was a fire truck.

Troy and Cindy live in a rural area of Maple Ridge, BC, and the firemen were the first responders. Our son Robert is a fireman at the responding fire station. Bobby was away on a fishing trip with his son Alec and his brother-in-law Jay, mercifully saving him from being first on scene to attend to his cousin. An ambulance was called. Confused and combative with the ambulance attendants and trying to sit up, Troy had to be restrained.

The weekend of the accident, Bob and I were at a neighborhood fundraiser in our hometown of Gibsons. Friends had helped organize a block party to raise funds to drill a borehole well in Malawi, Africa. In March the following year, we planned to travel with Roger, drill the well, and continue afterwards with a holiday. We wanted to see more of Malawi, and visit our daughter Michelle's, World Vision child.

Barbecued hot dogs, potato chips, and soft drinks are served at the fundraiser. A stellar August day, a live band donates its time, enlivening the festivities and a silent auction of generously donated gifts, adds to the funds raised. Friends roll up their sleeves. As a surprise, my younger sister Lorraine and her husband Dave, fly in from Edmonton. The block party is winding down so Lorraine, Dave, Bob, and I decide to go home, clean up and then return for a private party to follow.

We are just in the door at home when the telephone rings. It is Dennis and he is sobbing uncontrollably. "Troy has had an accident, we are on our way to the hospital, and they think he may not survive!" A sob catches in my throat and my knees buckle as I slump onto the bed. I try to reassure him. Dennis can be prone to exaggeration and I pray that this is one of those times. It is five o'clock in the afternoon. Bob and I decide to catch a late ferry to the mainland to be with Dennis, Carryl, and the rest of the family.

At the hospital, red-eyed family members clutching tattered Kleenex, line the walls outside the Intensive Care Unit. Carryl collapses into my arms sobbing, a shell of the person I know, unrecognizable. Normally, she is the stoic, the strong one, never drawing attention to herself, and never complaining. I babble, trying to console her, telling her stories of other people we know who have survived brain injuries; my niece Sandy, Michelle's ex father-in-law Jim, even a common nephew, Ben. I tell her it is not going to be easy, it took Sandy many surgeries and months of rehabilitation, and Jim, a year to recover to a semblance of his old self. She smiles briefly, hopeful, and says, "I could happily pamper and spoil Troy for a year, nurse him back to health." What I say next I come to regret, and still haunts me, "He will be alright. There is no other option, no other choice." However, Troy was not.

ICU lets two family members visit at a time and Dennis and Carryl encourage us to go in and see him. Bob and I respectfully decline; it is not a place for us now. It is a time for Dennis, Carryl, and Cindy. Thrust on display, it should be a private time for Jake and Sam, Troy's two young sons.

Bob's youngest brother, Tim, chooses to see Troy. A late baby in the family, Tim feels more like a brother to his nieces and nephews, than an uncle. Tim is big and burly. Shaved baldhead, tattooed arms, and a scruffy goatee, he wears a red sleeveless shirt stretched over his ample belly and loose fitting grey track pants. He walks with the unmistakable, 'Boileau swagger'. He is often mistaken as a biker, a Hell's Angel, but although he appears gruff and rough, he has a child-like demeanor and a marshmallow heart. After seeing Troy, Tim leans against the wall of the hospital corridor; his face blanches as he slides down into a heap on the floor losing consciousness.

Troy survives on a ventilator for three days as his brain continues to swell beyond the capacity of his skull. With severe anguish, the family decides to allow him a peaceful passing. Troy James Boileau was forty-one years old.

Troy's funeral is unbearable. Dennis, slightly obsessive compulsive, attends to every detail. Cindy chooses the church, or should I say, Troy chose the church. Eerily foreboding, after attending the funeral of a friend, Troy confided to Cindy, "If I die, this is the church where I want my funeral to be."

Cindy asks 'in lieu of flowers', people donate to '*The Eternal Life Project*'. Troy had become interested and excited when his twelve-year-old son Sam came home from school talking about this organization. '*The Eternal Life Project*' had often used the public schools as a forum to educate the children about Malawi,

Africa and to raise funds for its projects. Neither Troy nor Cindy was aware that *'The Eternal Life Project'* was a project of the society with which Bob and I had been to Africa. On the day of Troy's accident, we were raising funds at our block party for the project.

Incredibly, friends and family donate $ 20,955.47 to *'The Eternal Life Project'* in memory of Troy.

The following is an account of our trip to Malawi in March of 2009 as stewards of their extreme generosity, a special journey.

Troy's Well

"What we have done for ourselves alone dies with us; what we have done for others and the world remains and is immortal."
- Freemason, Albert Pike

Exhausted, after an arduous, thirty-five hour journey, we spend the night in the capital city of Lilongwe. Our rental vehicle, a Toyota Prado, solid and safe with new tires, will allow us to access the off road well sites. The windshield is cracked and the body has numerous scrapes and contusions. It will serve our purpose well.

After some quick business in town, we set out for Ntcheu. Bob drives cautiously at first, becoming accustomed to driving a strange vehicle on the left hand side of the road. Soon, we are cruising comfortably, down the straight and narrow roadway. The highway is two-way asphalt with jagged shoulders and deep potholes. Local traffic travels fast, belching puffs of black acrid smoke, leaving its carbon footprint.

As we motor, all of the reasons I am in love with Africa flood my heart. Malawi is healthy. It has been raining heavily for over a month and the rivers are swollen with swirling chalky muck. The day is clear; a soft baby blue sky is dotted with billowy, stark white, cotton-ball clouds. Pink, yellow, orange, and white wildflowers bloom in the long wheat coloured grasses in a landscape painted shades of luscious green. Ochre pathways crisscross fields, scarring a terrain rutted and hardened by thousands of pairs of flattened cracked feet. Villages of circular mud and stick rondevals nestle in the folds of verdant valleys.

People are everywhere, walking. Men, wearing dusty rumpled suit jackets, riding rusted tubular bicycles. Women, sarongs brilliantly contrasted against ebony skin, carry loads balanced on ramrod straight spines, postures a model would envy. Like beasts of burden, their heads are laden with plastic tubs, wicker baskets, tin buckets brimming with water, or awkward bundles of sticks tied with twine. Babies are swaddled on their backs.

Impromptu markets spring up at the edges of small villages. Crude fruit and vegetable stands, built of gnarled upright sticks with tin or thatched roofs, line the road. Tomatoes, potatoes, corn, and sweet potatoes piled in perfect pyramids, atop tin plates, await customers.

We arrive to a warm welcome, embraced like distant relatives returning for a family visit. The Angoni Beverly Hills Villas have undergone some improvements since our last visit. James shows us to a new updated room. It is round and large with a polished concrete floor, covered with a patchwork of faded carpet remnants. A king sized bed fills the centre of the room and thankfully, has a firm foam mattress. The shower, constructed of red brick, has a 220-volt electric showerhead; the type that reminds you periodically that water and electricity are never a good mix. It dribbles body temperature water if left running long enough before getting in.

After we settle in, James and Marian are eager to show us the orphan care centre. Under construction for the past five weeks, it is in the tiny village of Chinyamula, directly behind the well, which 'The Eternal Life Project', drilled last fall. Monies donated in memory of our nephew, funded the building. Roger will install a photo in the feeding center. In the picture, from Troy's obituary, he has a playful smile on his face, and standing in front of a bar-b-que, he is holding a plateful of food; a fitting picture.

Constructed of red brick, on a solid, raised, concrete foundation, the building has a shiny corrugated tin roof and a stone fireplace with a brick chimney. A storage room, to house bags of maize and dried beans, sits at one end. The feeding centre will prepare meals for over one hundred orphans.

The construction crew is on site and our presence attracts the attention of several of the village women and children. During construction, the sand and gravel for the building was dumped at the well site and as the rainy season monsoons fell, the women packed full buckets four hundred feet to the building site where the men mixed cement.

Eight village women sit straight legged in the dirt at the edge of a vegetable garden, flourishing because of the new well. Their heads are wrapped in vivid scarves; their skin prematurely aged by the African sun. As we prepare to leave, I ask James, "How do you say goodbye in Chichewa?" I turn, addressing the women, *"Khalawi Bwino."* They spontaneously burst into a soulful a cappella song. "They are singing God bless you, God bless you for what you have done," James interprets. Thinking of Troy, tears well in my eyes.

On May 19[th,] the people of Malawi will go to the polls in a general election. One of the candidates running for president is John Tembo. James Logan owns the Villa where we are staying in Ntcheu. James's son, Terrance is running on Tembo's docket. Now, try to follow me. James Logan was instrumental in choosing the sites for our two new wells. These sites are, coincidentally, located in Terrance's ridings.

Politics in Africa are serious. Riots happen. People are maimed and killed by crazed marauding mobs wielding machetes. We purposely plan our trip to be in and out of Malawi, before the election when political temperatures could reach the flash point.

The day before we are to drill well number one, Terrance arrives at the Villa. He is impeccably dressed and driving a flashy red pick-up truck with shiny chrome hubcaps. We are aware of his presence but he keeps his distance, conferring in privacy with his father. Terrance leaves early the next morning. James also leaves early to head to the well site, to meet the drilling rig. Unbeknownst to us, the timing is all carefully planned.

The previous night, James tells us he will go to the site and set up the rig and he will call us in the afternoon to let us know when we should come. "No need for you to be there all day in the hot sun," he says. What we didn't realize is that Terrance has also gone to the well site, to campaign. He hands out multi-coloured cotton wraps to the women, called *chintenje*, with his name and face emblazoned on them, and we assume, mounts the soapbox. Campaigning, he takes credit for the fact that the well is being provided in their village.

Back at the villa, after lunch, we pile into the Toyota and head south towards Balaka. From the back seat, Marian instructs Bob to turn off the paved highway. For fifteen kilometers, we bump down the narrow rutted road, branches scratching the vehicle.

When we arrive, Terrance is long gone. However, the festivities continue for our benefit.

The well site buzzes with activity. People have walked from far corners to watch. The drillers are inserting the last section of rod. Milk chocolate water spews high in the air. Women sing, giving thanks, as barefooted children in soiled tattered clothes, run and laugh. An elderly man leans on a bicycle laden with sugar cane. A young man, in a chain driven, bicycle tired, wheel chair, negotiates over the rough terrain. Young men talk, sitting on the brick remnants of an abandoned project. Women sit in a circle chatting, peeling kernels of maize from cobs into a basket. My camera, as always, is an instant attraction. The children push and shove to be the next to have their pictures taken. I stop often, relocating myself, to prevent a mini riot. The people are beautiful, warm, and welcoming. Three grandmothers approach me, a grey haired delegation, they chatter in Chichewa affectionately clutching my hand. "I'm sorry, I don't understand you," I apologize, however their chatter continues unabated. They include me, a new girlfriend, into their intimate circle.

A carnival atmosphere pervades; kids run everywhere and women sing. The children join in the songs, small black hands clapping to the rhythm. I clap along mimicking the words. "What are the children singing," I ask Marian. "They are praising Logan, giving thanks to Logan, Logan." Then Marian adds something I remember clearly later that night, "But not everyone here is in favor of him and will give him their vote."

That night, in bed at the villa, I wake for my nightly pee and a realization hits me like the proverbial, 'ton of bricks'. We have just taken part in a political rally. "Bob, are you awake?" "Yes," he grumbles. "I was just thinking about what happened today." "What?" "We are in Africa and we are extremely visible." "We have just endorsed a politician who may not be popular with some people." "We may have, unwittingly, put ourselves in danger."

I envision the headline: *'CANADIAN COUPLE, DOING HUMANITARIAN WORK IN MALAWI, KIDNAPPED AND KILLED BY MILITANT MOB'.*

I am so distressed and agitated that I actually convince Bob we should catch the first available flight out in the morning. Thankfully, my paranoia subsides, and ebbs with the rising sun.

The water springing forth from *'Troy's Well'* will be lifesaving and life giving. We will return in a day or two, when they install the cement trough, to mount a granite plaque. We carried the plaque on the plane, guarding it carefully. Thanks to Joe, Bob's brother, for wrapping it up carefully, it survived the trip intact. The plaque is an etched black granite tile with gold lettering, a cross in one corner, and a Canadian flag in the other.

Prior to Troy's death, we fund-raised to drill a well. Funds and support came from friends, family and perfect strangers. Friends donated garage sale items and we held a successful

Troy's Well

neighborhood block party. We are humbled by the trust and faith, and we shall be eternally grateful.

Well number two proves to be a little more difficult. The drillers sink thirteen sections of three-meter long pipe, hitting water, but the well fails to pump for more than five minutes. James convinces them that it is not enough and insists they relocate and try again. They are just pulling the pipes back up when we arrive. We stand in the hot afternoon sun among a crowd of onlookers. The rig relocates and begins drilling. The compressor sprays a loud gust of air and squealing frightened villagers scatter, like a cobra has suddenly made its way into their midst. As the drill digs into the dry ground white clouds of dust swirl coating our teeth with a fine filmy layer. Nine pipes grind into the arid earth as we watch in anticipation. Perhaps the next pipe will hit water, nothing but dust. We need to leave; Roger has arranged to meet Stanley back at the hotel at six o'clock. It is disheartening to leave without seeing water.

We are no sooner back at the villa, when James calls to say they have hit water, and lots of it. Thank the gods.

Late the next afternoon, word arrives that the men are starting the cement trough and wash sinks at 'Troy's Well'. The granite plaque needs to be imbedded in the wet cement. James has built a box to form a raised platform for the plaque.

When we arrive, the forms are installed and most of the red bricks forming the double sinks are in. Chipped pieces of red brick provide a rocky base where the concrete will be poured. The men are starting to mix cement. They have a pile of sand and a pile of golf ball-size gravel, crushed by hand with a small sledgehammer.

Installing the Plaque

Two barrels of water stand to one side filled by three young girls with the heavy pails balanced precariously on their heads.

James's form is placed at the base of the pump's pipe stand, under where the extension of the pump handle will be mounted. A perfect place, the plaque will be shielded from damage by the pump handle and be in a place of prominence. The young workmen place the plaque carefully and respectfully, aware of its importance. James explains to them in Chichewa the story behind the plaque. They nod somberly as I weep. Tenderly wiping smudged cement from the surface, they cover it in cardboard and bubble wrap, to protect it as cement is shoveled around it.

The well will be ready for use in one week's time, after the concrete has had ample time to cure. We will return to see a bucket of lifesaving clear clean water pump from *'Troy's Well'*. Rest peacefully Troy, we love you.

Bob and I clasp hands and looking skyward, we send a big thank-you to everyone who has helped the well become a reality and for all of their loving care and warm support. Our hearts and thoughts are with Cindy, Jake, Sam, Carryl, Dennis, Tammy, Cory, and all of the friends and family who have wrapped them in their loving arms.

Black Market Money

The following scary story, resulting in lost sleep, happens the very next night.

When Roger comes to Malawi, he brings cash in American dollars. He exchanges the money on the 'Black Market' because the banks in Malawi will give him one hundred and forty-one Malawian Kwacha for each American dollar, as opposed to the 'Black Market', where he will get one hundred and seventy-two

Malawian Kwacha, for each American dollar. This is a difference too large to ignore and Roger being frugal with every penny of donated money, feels it is a risk worth taking.

The purchasing of Black Market monies is common practice in Malawi and the transaction can be done at most hotels and in the parking lots of most markets. Sleazy moneychangers slouch against the concrete walls of the supermarket chatting casually, awaiting customers.

Roger needs to exchange ten thousand American dollars to have enough Kwacha to pay the well drillers. We are all nervous about exchanging the large amount. We are in a visible rental vehicle and if we do the exchange at the market in Lilongwe and then drive to Ntcheu, we know that we will be lucky to survive for fifty kilometers unscathed.

Roger connives a plan. Stanley, the manager for the Korea Garden Lodge, tells Roger that for fifty American dollars and a tank of gas, he will deliver the Kwacha from Lilongwe to Ntcheu, a distance of approximately one hundred and sixty-eight kilometers. All Roger has to do is to call him and let him know when he wants it.

Roger calls Stanley and asks if he can deliver the money the following day, Friday. "I can't on Friday but I can bring it to you tonight around six p.m. if that is okay," replies Stanley.

The meeting with Stanley forced us to leave the site of well number two while it was still spewing dust. Supper is finished and Stanley has not yet arrived. At eight p.m., our cell phone rings. Stanley is in the parking lot of the Villa. Bob and Roger find him standing beside a small compact car. He is with three companions and Bob and Roger suspect that they are armed.

"Where do you want to do this?" Stanley asks Bob. "Come into our room," Bob replies. The scene is straight out of a B grade spy movie. Stanley and one of his henchmen slouch on chairs in our room. They extract heavy bricks of Kwacha from a black duffle bag. Three bricks of 500,000 Kwacha each and 272,000 bundled in 10,000 kwacha packets wrapped in elastic bands, 1.72 million. (Some information you need to know is that the largest Kwacha note is five hundred and equivalent to approximately three American dollars!)

Roger hands Stanley five white vellum envelopes each holding two thousand American dollars in crisp one hundred dollar bills. Stanley hands the envelopes off to his henchman who hastily counts the bills. He crumples the envelopes into balls, depositing them on the floor of our room, and then stuffs the bills into the pockets of his baggy pants.

Our business done, suddenly the focus in the room shifts. Stanley spots our net laundry bag full of inflated soccer balls. His face breaks into a broad toothy grin, "Can I have one of your soccer balls? I have a team." Bob glances sideways in my direction. What could we say? The two men bounce each of the regulation-sized balls, spinning them around on large palms, searching for the best specimen. Two are chosen. "Sorry fellows, one is all you get," I snarl. I am determined to deposit the rest of them into the hands of children.

1.72 Million Kwacha
– Black Market Money

Exchange done and hands shaken, Stanley and the henchman exit our room.

When they leave, Bob, Roger and I are giddy. We stack up the bills on the bed and a small end table snapping pictures, laughing with a nervous hysteria.

Roger retires to his room. Two of the 500,000 Kwacha stacks are wrapped in plastic with a yellow piece of paper on one end. I joke to Bob, "Maybe there are just bills on the top and the bottom and the centre is filled with newspaper." Bob snickers nervously, however we both check to ensure the bills are solid all the way through. Bob and I stuff the stacks into our big suitcase and lock it up for the night.

My eyes spring open in the middle of the night. I whisper, "Are you awake?" "Yes." "You realize what we have just done don't you?" "What now?" he enquires testily. "I know Roger trusts Stanley but he has three, likely armed, guys with him whom we don't know. What if they decide to come back and kick down our door in the middle of the night and rob us?" Unconcerned, Bob rolls away from me, "We will be fine, we are safe here. Go back to sleep."

Shit, another sleepless night!

A week later, when we are back in the Lilongwe, I convey this story to Melody over dinner. Melody has been working in the capital of Lilongwe for eight months and we are fortunate to be able to connect with her again. She assures me that my paranoia is founded. She is incredulous, "You guys, are you crazy? Ten thousand dollars is like a million dollars here!"

The Bonus

Two bonuses result from our trip this year to Malawi.

One bonus is reconnecting with our friend Melody, a friend we met in Zanzibar in 2006. Volunteering for Peace Corp, she was stationed in Nata Village in Botswana; however, she has since relocated to Lilongwe, the capital city of Malawi. We see Roger off on his flight back home to Canada and then call Melody on her cell phone. Map and directions in hand we head across the bridge from 'Old Town' Lilongwe, down Kenyatta Boulevard, towards city center. Melody lives on a road of large gated properties. Solid red brick fences, topped with Bougainvillea laced spikes, surround manicured lawns. Sentries, in phone booth-sized shacks, guard heavy steel gates. The large corrugated 'Vote for Obama' sign on the boulevard indicates that we have found the correct house. We honk twice and Melody's uniformed guard, Alice, saunters out of her guard shack leaning her shoulder into the heavy gate and rolling it back to let us pass.

Melody is living in the home of an ex-mayor of Lilongwe. A long single story red brick rancher, the house has seen better days and is in a state of gradual disrepair. Carpets have been stripped exposing a polished concrete floor. The large home has two bathrooms, both with perpetually leaky toilets. Melody has invited friends for cocktails, some colleagues from Peace Corp, as well as other aid organizations; a kindred bunch drawn together by common interests and goals whose families are far away and do not understand. In her early fifties, Melody is one of the older volunteers and the younger ones often rely on her for motherly advice.

Melody's time in Malawi has broken her spirit and she visibly sags as she greets us. The corruption is rife and millions of dollars of aid money is not getting to the people who need it most. She is counting down the days on pages of calendars taped crudely in her hallway; big black exes and a prisoner's lament, ninety left. She is convinced that her soul will be destroyed first. Our visit temporarily uplifts her and before we leave, she gets word that she has been accepted to a new job, a paid position with Peace Corp, in Turkmenistan. She is elated but could it be a case of 'be careful what you wish for'?

The second bonus to our trip is the opportunity to visit Jefrey. Our daughter Michelle and her family, sponsor Jefrey through World Vision Canada. As a family, they scanned the World Vision website looking for the right child, Michelle holding back tears, wishing she could choose them all. They chose Malawi because we have been there and they chose Jefrey because he is cute. Jefrey is five years old.

Michelle decided to sponsor a child as a lesson of giving and to teach her children to appreciate the life they are fortunate to live, and "Hey Mom, I can afford thirty-five dollars a month to help a less fortunate child."

Michelle's children enjoy getting Jefrey's picture and penciled letters, translated into English by an older boy. They are thrilled when they find out that we will travel to his village to visit and to 'check' on him for them.

A Love Letter to Our Grandchildren

Dearest Wesley, Marenda, and Kaiden:

Papa and I want to thank-you for giving us the opportunity to visit your little World Vision brother in Malawi, Africa. We had an awesome time today with Jefrey and his family!

The village where Jefrey lives is far off the highway on a bumpy dusty red dirt road. It took us forty-five minutes to drive there from the World Vision office.

First, we visited the Clinic where Jefrey will go to see a doctor if he is sick. The lady from World Vision, Maureena, explains to us that if Jefrey needs to go to a hospital he will be able to go to a Catholic Mission Hospital nearby because your family sponsors him and therefore, World Vision will pay for his care. The nurses at the clinic weigh the little kids on a big scale like the one you would see in a butcher shop. The kids hang by a harness on a big meat hook while the nurse writes their weight in their charts. The charts are kept in decorated laminated file folders, one for each child. Tracking growth and weight of the children is important because so many of the children have poor nutrition and fail to thrive.

Maureena tells us Jefrey is a lucky boy because few sponsors visit World Vision children in Malawi.

After the clinic, we are off to the school where we finally get to meet Jefrey. When we arrive at the school the older children are standing on a small hill and holding up big poster-sized signs saying, *'Robert and Rosalie You are Most Welcome'* and *'Welcome to Mkwawra*

Meeting Jefrey

School'. The kids are singing and clapping. Maureena says their song is saying, "Thankyou for coming, we should put our two hands together in thanks". Hundreds of children greet us.

Jefrey is alone, sitting at a desk inside the school, waiting for us. I am sure he is as nervous about meeting us as we are about meeting him. The minute I see him, I recognize him from the pictures you have of him at home. He has just celebrated his eighth birthday and he is so cute. He is tiny for an eight-year-old. Jefrey has a shaved head and huge brown eyes rimmed with ebony lashes. Quick to smile, his mouth is filled with straight white teeth. Jefrey is the 'Prince for the Day' and he knows it.

We give the school five soccer balls, two big crank-style pencil sharpeners and two sets of laminated maps; one is a map of the world and one a map of Canada. We show all of the children where Malawi is, where Canada is, and where your family lives. The children are amazed that we would come so far just to see them.

As we leave the school, hundreds of children run behind the World Vision truck, creating a giant dust cloud with their bare feet. Jefrey and his two older brothers have the honour of riding in the World Vision truck ahead of us.

We drive deep into the village to Jefrey's home, which is built of red bricks mortared with mud. The roof is dried grass and sunbeams shine through it onto the hard packed dirt floor. The house has one small window with a small wooden door but no

At Jefrey's School

glass. The entire house is the size of one of your bedrooms.

We are welcomed in and sit on a bamboo mat on the floor. It fills the entire living area; there is no furniture. Two small bedrooms, with cloth sheets covering the doorways, sit off to the side of the living area. One bedroom is for mom and dad and the other bedroom is for Jefrey and the two smaller children, Ruthness three, and Mike six. Jefrey's two older brothers live nearby at their Auntie's house because Jefrey's house is too small for the whole family.

The gifts we bring, from you guys, fill the entire house. A big blue plastic basin holds cooking oil, rice, sugar, salt, maize (corn), hot chocolate (this made everyone smile), powdered milk, a big bag of suckers, juice mix, laundry soap, hand soap, toothpaste, toothbrushes and lots of other goodies. We bring them a gas lantern, candles, matches, a cooler, and a kettle. The day, for them, was like the best Christmas or Birthday you can remember! All of the kids get a ball and other treats, and we give Ruthness a baby doll. I shopped the entire city looking for a black baby doll but there was none to be found. The one I did find is dressed in a pink sleeper and it cries when you squeeze it. Ruthness is scared to touch the doll and her eyes widen with fear when it cries. I hope, given time, she will warm up to it.

Jefrey is overjoyed when he gets his backpack full of the stuff you sent. Everyone laughs when I put the elephant mask on him for a picture and he refuses to let go of the 'glow-in-the-dark' soccer ball, his favorite gift. He loves his sunglasses and keeps them on for the rest of the day. His eyes light up when he sees the matchbox cars and he generously passes one of them to one of his older brothers. We know everything in the backpack will be shared and that is good. One of the biggest kids in the room is Mom. I caught her several times gently lofting a yellow balloon in the air, with a soft serene smile on her face. When I looked her way, she appeared shy and embarrassed and passed the balloon over to baby Ruthness.

With Maureena interpreting, we talk a lot about you guys. They really enjoy the pictures of the snow you sent. None of them have ever seen snow and probably, never will. Nana's eyes overflow with tears when I am handed a picture of your family, the one of all of you that was taken at your school. It is wrinkled, worn, and tattered, by all of their loving hands.

Remember, none of the family speaks any English. We do have Maureena with us to translate but the best part is that love needs no language, just like a baby knows its mother loves it even though it can't understand the words she is cooing. A special time for us, and all of you, you were all here in Jefrey's little home today.

After our time with the family, we all load into the World Vision trucks and drive about forty-five minutes into town for lunch, at 'Joe's Motel'. It is quite an event for the family. Maureena says many of the people in the villages live their entire lives there, never getting the chance to leave. We all have big meals, a choice of roasted chicken or goat stew with rice or nsima (a sticky white lump made out of maize) and some spinach. Papa has the chicken, I have the goat stew, and it is yummy. The kids love their lemon 'Fanta' sodas, and Mom and Dad drink Coca-Colas.

After lunch, the family piles into the back of the World Vision truck for their trip back into the village. It is difficult to watch them leave. Nana just wants to gather them all up in her arms and smother them with kisses but I would have scared the heck out of all of them! As the family climbs into the truck, I can see soft blue warmth connecting you in Canada with Jefrey's family in Africa and I feel like Papa and I are the link.

It is important that you understand something. Jefrey is poor; there is no doubt about that, however he is happy and healthy and has a family and a village who cares deeply for him. There is no need to feel sorry for him.

Wesley, Marenda, Kaiden, Mommy and Daddy, you are making a big difference in the life of a sweet little boy who lives a world away but will never forget you.

When I was a little girl, my Father taught me an important but simple lesson. He would say, "Always remember, in this world no one is any better than you are. However, you are no better than anyone else." We all walk the same path.

The Warm Heart of Africa

Malawi is a small country that is situated where the heart would be if Africa were a living entity. We decide to explore some of the country, eventually making our way to the lake. Lake Malawi comprises one third of the small country and we have yet to see it. We hope for tourist filled resorts, sandy beaches, and a reprieve from the poverty.

The rain will not stop and we are concerned about road conditions as we motor south. The police have the road blocked as we near Nkhotakhota. Vehicles line the side of the highway; a small bus, a huge overland safari bus filled with tourists, several mini buses, and numerous cars. A crowd is gathering; women with babies swaddled and cargo on their heads, men on bicycles, children splashing in the puddles, isolated groups of tough teenage boys, girls holding hands and giggling. A policeman dressed in army fatigues, polished high top leather boots and a green pith helmet, approaches Bob's open window. "The road is closed," he states. "Is it too deep to go through?" Bob enquires. "You see, the problem is, there are several turns in the road and if you do not know it well, you will sink. Perhaps if you wait for a while, the water will go down enough, and you can proceed."

Bob shuts off the truck and we mingle with the growing crowd. A few brave souls wade their way thigh deep in the swirling floodwaters. A few push bicycles, successfully making their way to the other side where a similar crowd is waiting on the rise of a small hill. One minibus crosses from the far side as the passengers flank either side, guiding it. The crowd cheers.

After an hour of waiting, the overland safari bus decides to attempt a crossing. The driver fires up his diesel engine and Bob follows suit, deciding to follow closely in his wake. The tourists hang out of the windows snapping photos. The behemoth truck shudders with the force of the roaring floodwaters. A wide waterfall gushes as it overflows the edge of the asphalt. The crowd cheers us on. My heart pounds in my chest as we cross the watery expanse.

Malawi continues to challenge us. Signage is poor or non-existent, the roads are horrendous, and our guidebook is virtually useless.

Mua Mission, run by a French Canadian priest named Father Boucher, is our destination for today. With the help of the mission, the village has built six small chalet cottages at the edge of the Mua River that they rent out to tourists. The cottages are simple but clean, with en-suite washrooms. Tasty and filling set meals are served in a small dining room.

It is Saturday afternoon and the small museum is closed. We meet an elderly English couple, also staying the night. Their guide finds someone who will open the museum and give the four of us a private guided tour. Mike is full of information about the history of the mission and is an excellent storyteller. I ask him if the people resented the missionaries bringing their religion. He was gracious and explained, "At first, yes. They preached to us in Latin and we didn't understand Latin." Then he said something astounding, "You know, we worship the same God. We just get to him on different pathways." He went on to explain, "For instance, if you are walking towards me, you see my front," he says, sweeping his hands head to foot at his side. "But if someone is walking behind me, they see my back. I look different to both of you, but I am still the same person."

After dinner, we sit outside on the concrete steps watching from above, as on the opposite riverbank, the villagers gather for evening ablutions. Women, bent at the waist, scrub laundry on rough boulders and then *thwack, thwack, thwack* the rolled up clothes to extract the water. If I close my eyes, I swear I am listening to the chopping of firewood. Small children cavort naked in the deep pools, bath time and playtime. Young girls walk up the steep slippery bank to the thatch-roofed village, carrying pails of water atop their heads. Babies cry, goats bleat and the smell of cooking fires permeate the air. Upstream, the men bathe alone.

Early morning, before the sun rises to warm the earth, the rhythmic *thwack, thwack, thwack* wakes me.

It is the Sunday before Easter, Palm Sunday. An old brick bridge crosses the river and as we approach, villagers are crossing in the opposite direction, dressed in their Sunday finest. A white priest, clad in white vestments with a red sash, stands slightly elevated above the crowd, his hands clasped at his waist. Children and young people sing hymns as the young priest looks on. Altar boys emerge from the church behind us dressed in red and white robes and carrying tall white candles. Nuns in drab navy-blue habits approach us and clasp our hands in welcome. Watching at the sidelines, we marvel at the reverence of the open-air service as God shoots sunbeams through the tree branches to halo the parishioners.

Onwards to Cape Maclear, a tourist Mecca on Lake Malawi. Surely here, we will find our sandy beaches and tourist resorts. Not so! The cape is eighteen kilometers off the highway. Once again, we rattle around in the cab of our vehicle, bouncing unmercifully down the dusty potholed road.

Town is a bumpy dirt strip two kilometers long, divided by majestic baobab trees, and running the length of the bay through a small village. We are disoriented. Young men jump in front of our vehicle trying to persuade us towards one resort or another. Gangs of children shout *muzungu* (white man) and bumper ride until Bob slams on the brakes and they scatter like rats.

We decide to splurge and treat ourselves. A company, Kayak Africa, owns two small islands situated off shore. One, Mumbo Island, has six luxury safari tents perched on rock ledges. Mumbo Island is very expensive but it is the off-season and they offer us a reduced rate. Everything, other than the bar tab, is included in the price. We are ferried over to the island in a crude wooden water taxi.

Our tent, heavy canvas under a thatch-roofed structure, is on a rocky outcropping overlooking the turquoise bay. Two beds, with crisp linen sheets, fill the tent. A large covered deck extends out front with a hammock and two cushioned wicker chairs. No electricity. At dusk, staff brings paraffin lanterns to light the eco-friendly washrooms and walkways. The washroom is in a separate bamboo screened open structure. A bucket equipped with a showerhead is filled with steaming water on request. Waves rhythmically lap onto the coarse sandy beach.

Bob and I absorb the luxury; these comforts are temporary and every moment precious. We do as little as possible and as much as possible. Snorkeling in the lake with the iridescent cichlids, we knowingly risk Bilharzias (a boring parasite carried by the snails that inhabit the lake). We hike the crisscrossing trails scaring huge monitor lizards from hidey-holes. After warm showers, we sit on our deck sipping cold wine; knowing full well that tomorrow will come too soon. I awake at one in the morning to a tent flooded with a soft orange glow from a full African moon.

Sucked back to reality and on a mission, we travel the highway north of Balaka, turning off onto a dusty back road. We have come to check both of the well sites.

Our first stop is the second well drilled, the one that was spouting dust the last time we were there. An elderly lady greets us, "*Zikomo*," she says as she clutches my hand. The well is complete, the concrete trough and sinks finished. A few pumps of the handle produces water. We are pleased.

At *'Troy's Well'*, the situation is different. We are deflated; there is no pump handle on the well. A white sack is tied over the pump head and branches with spiky prickles surround the concrete trough. Coarse sand is scattered on the fresh smooth concrete. Arid and barren it shows no signs of the *'Eternal Life'* we promised. I am nauseous; my heart is heavy in my chest.

When we arrive at the Logan's, James is surprised to learn that the well is not operating. He calls his son Terrance to investigate. That evening Terrance knocks on our door and assures us that, the handle will be installed in the morning. The chief has the handle and has been away.

The following morning we are not surprised to see that nothing has been done. "Should we call James?" I ask Bob. "What for?" he grouses. "Let's look for the chief." We stop three ladies passing the soccer field, "Do you know where the chief lives?" They answer in Chichewa. Bob pumps his fist up and down, up and down. "Eh," they answer in unison, pointing to a small brick house behind the field.

Tinny music emanates from the yard. I stay in the vehicle as Bob disappears into the yard. Five minutes pass and he emerges with a young man named Robert, who tells us that the pump handle is in the house but that the man who has the key is in the field working. "Can you come back tomorrow?" Robert asks. "No! The handle will go on today!" Bob declares. "The people will be happy. The village has suffered without water for a long time," Robert reports. Robert jumps into the back seat and we head off looking for 'the man with the key'. Three kilometers back towards the highway, Robert instructs Bob to stop at a broad pathway where he sprints barefoot into the cornfield. Fifteen minutes later, he returns smiling, with 'the man with the key'.

Back at the well, Bob pulls the prickly branches away from the trough. A young girl hands me a whiskbroom of grass tied with twine and I brush the sand away around the plaque. A woman takes the broom from my hand and finishes the job. Moments

The First Water from 'Troy's Well'

later, Robert and several of the village men, emerge from the bush carrying the pump handle. Villagers are gathering. Bob removes the sack from the wellhead and the handle is cranked into place. Up, down, up, down, up, down, a nervous laugh of relief bursts from Bob as the 'water of life' spurts forth from the spout.

Waiting for Water

A pubescent girl waits patiently on the sidelines. A green bar of soap sits on short-cropped hair atop her head and a green toothbrush juts sideways out of her mouth. She giggles, embarrassed, as I snap her photo.

CHAPTER 20

Roatan, Bay Islands – Honduras – Central America

The Colombians and the Cobras

March of 2010, on a moonless night and under a veil of darkness, seven speedboats race along the Honduran coast. The occupants are heavily armed and carry a valuable cargo, over twelve million dollars of baled cocaine. From the jungles of Colombia, the cocaine is destined for Mexico. As the boats near the reef at the east end of Roatan, close to the island of St. Helene, one of their engines suffers mechanical failure and has to be towed into the safety of the harbour. Six of the speedboats continue their journey; the broken down boat and its valuable cargo is left guarded.

Local thugs from Diamond Rock, who hear news of the breakdown, seize the opportunity to steal the booty. This action launches an all out drug war.

The first we hear of the trouble, on the east end of the island, is the following day when we are having lunch at 'The Bakery' in French Harbour. Jane from 'The Bakery' chats with us at our table, "Have you heard about what is happening in Diamond Rock. They are under siege. Friends of mine were driving the potholed road in their pickup truck and they had to abandon it and run for their lives when they were caught in the crossfire!" "What?" I spit out.

Rumours run rampant on the island. The police are not equipped to deal with the situation; the Colombians out gun them. Special Forces police called Cobras are sent over from the mainland, but they too, are hopelessly ill equipped. Roadblocks are set up but the police are forced to let the fray run its course. Bad guys are killing bad guys, however the situation soon escalates into something more serious.

After a week has passed, Bob and I decide to brave a trip out to Marble Hills Farms for lunch. Marble Hills is quite a bit of distance before Diamond Rock and although we are on high alert, we feel it will be safe enough to venture out.

Rebecca, the waitress at Marble Hills, eagerly fills us in on the latest news. "Oh yeah, I spent two days here afraid to go home. My mother called me and told me to stay put it wasn't safe. Two houses had grenades thrown into them burning them to the ground, and in one of them, a woman and a teenage boy died. One of our dive boats and our boat captain has been missing for three days now." " Was he involved?" I enquire incredulous. She shrugs her shoulders and replies, "We don't know, but he IS a Bailey," as if it answers my query.

In early February of 2011, a friend told me that the boat captain from Marble Hills had, indeed, been found. At least, part of him was;

his severed head was found on the driver's seat of his pickup truck. The truck was parked in Diamond Rock and left as a warning!

Throughout the week, the rumours get more outrageous with stories of headless limbless torsos washing up on Camp Bay beach. Two Italian businessmen from the West end of the island disappear; both of them last seen together in a red car. Are they part of this? It is speculated that they sold the drugs for the boys from Diamond Rock making a huge profit and then disappeared from Roatan voluntarily, back to safety in Italy. Family members on the island and back in Italy claim no knowledge of their disappearance and fear that they are dead.

One of the missing Italians, Maurilio Mirabella owner of Waihuka Adventure Divers on Roatan, has been headlined in the news in the past. The following is an Internet account of an incident 'caught on tape' by one of the divers present the day the incident happened. Open-mouthed we viewed the grainy footage on a television in a room of one of the local hotels.

Roatan shark feeder charged with attempted murder

By LAMAR BENNINGTON @ CDNN - CYBER DIVER News Network

ROATAN, Honduras (25 Feb 2009) — A shark feeding profiteer in Roatan has been charged with attempted murder.

Waihuka Adventure Divers owner Maurilio Mirabella, who sells shark feeding dives to thrill-seeking tourists, allegedly attacked a competing dive operator underwater at a shark-feeding site near Roatan's airport.

Witnesses said Mirabella attacked Willie DeBeer, a Sueño del Mar dive guide who took a group of tourists to the shark feeding site.

Mirabella, apparently attempting to prevent a competing dive operator from profiting off of "his sharks," tried to shut off DeBeer's air supply.

DeBeer fought off the initial attack but the two PADI scuba diving instructors continued to scuffle as horrified scuba diving tourists looked on in shock and disbelief.

DeBeer survived the violent attack and reported the incident to authorities who have charged Mirabella with attempted murder.

Mirabella has declined to comment on the charges but said he sells shark feeding dives because "without sharks, scuba diving in Roatan isn't worth much.

Three weeks after the Columbian incident, Bob and I decide to drive out to Camp Bay. We have never been there and decide it will be a nice drive and a chance to explore more of the island.

Lunching at Camp Bay Beach Adventure Lodge, we are the only patrons. The woman who owns the Lodge chats with us at our table, "It is pretty safe here now," she says, "the Cobras were in here last week and I let them search the place and then fed them lunch." Then she tells us, "Occasionally, a bale of cocaine washes up on the beach here in Camp Bay and one of the locals finds it and sells it back to the Colombians. You will see them suddenly driving a new pickup. They call it 'finding their luck'."

Have I Settled?

The year is 2011, how can it be? Sometimes I feel old age, like a freight train, racing towards me.

This is our third winter spent in our new home. I can no longer describe it as a house it has become our home.

Every evening, Bob and I settle in two white plastic deck chairs facing the Caribbean Sea. Our wine glasses perspire, forming wet puddles as they warm in the evening sun. I swear I can hear a sizzle as we watch the sun sink into a horizon visible only because the sky is a softer shade of blue than the ocean. We talk; we always seem to have something to share, and we often touch hands.

I worry about having settled, staying too long in one spot, and I long to get back on an unknown road, an untraveled path. However, I think that it is only a well-deserved, and temporary rest.

My dear friend Melody reassures me, "You haven't settled. You are just doing something different."

We will see what the next chapter brings.

Epilogue

As much as we wish, we cannot alter our past, and we cannot foresee our future. It is imperative that we live in the now and move forward in life utilizing all of our six senses:

...The *TASTE* of sun ripened strawberries, fine Belgian chocolate, bubbly French champagne, or creamery ice cream.

...The *TOUCH* of fine silk, of sunbeams on naked skin, of soft kisses, or of a baby's bottom.

...The *SMELL* of an Indian spice market, of a puppy's breath, of the jungle after a tropical rain, or of your lover's pillow.

...The *SOUND* of an operatic aria, of songbirds in the springtime, of waves gently lapping the shore, or of a baby's first cry.

...The *SIGHT* of a soaring eagle, of a fiery sunset, of a daughter on her wedding day, or of a grandchild's first step.

...The *SPIRIT* of an awakening dawn, of a snow capped mountain reflecting on a moraine lake, of comforting a dying friend, or of the ghostly touch of a deceased parent.

I think myself an atheist, however words like blessed, spiritual, pray, and God incessantly creep their way into my vocabulary. When I was a child I was confounded by the concept of infinity, and I still am. Perhaps there is more. I certainly hope so.

Made in the USA
Charleston, SC
13 November 2011